Advanced Digital Imaging Laboratory Using MATLAB®

Advanced Digital Imaging Laboratory Using MATLAB®

Leonid P Yaroslavsky

Professor Emeritus, School of Electrical Engineering,
Tel Aviv University, Tel Aviv, Israel

IOP Publishing, Bristol, UK

ISBN   978-0-750-31050-5 (ebook)
ISBN   978-0-750-31051-2 (print)

DOI   10.1088/978-0-750-31050-5

Version: 20140701

IOP Expanding Physics
ISSN 2053-2563 (on-line)
ISSN 2054-7315 (print)

British Library Cataloguing-in-Publication Data: A catalogue record for this book is available from the British Library.

Published by IOP Publishing, wholly owned by The Institute of Physics, London

IOP Publishing, Temple Circus, Temple Way, Bristol, BS1 6HG, UK

US Office: IOP Publishing, The Public Ledger Building, Suite 929, 150 South Independence Mall West, Philadelphia, PA 19106, USA

Contents

Preface

This book is a textbook of MATLAB®-based exercises in all major topics of digital imaging: image digitization, digital image formation and computational imaging, image resampling and building continuous image models, image statistical characterization and noise diagnostics, statistical image models and pattern formation, image correlators for the detection and localization of objects, image restoration and perfecting, and image enhancement. The book is addressed to students, researchers and practitioners in imaging engineering and applications. Its goal is to help readers to master digital imaging on both fundamental theoretical and practical levels. It is based on courses that have been taught by the author at Tel Aviv University and at a number of other universities in Europe and Japan during the last 15 years.

Author biography

Leonid P Yaroslavsky

Leonid P Yaroslavsky, MS (summa cum laude, 1961), PhD (1968),
Dr Sc. Habilitatus in Physics and Math (1982), OSA Fellow. From 1965 till 1983,
the head of the Digital Image Processing and Digital Holography Group at the
Institute for Information Transmission Problems (IITP), Russian Academy of
Sciences. From 1983 till 1995, the founder and head of the Laboratory of Digital
Optics at the IITP. From 1995 till 2008, a full professor at the Faculty of
Engineering, Tel Aviv University. Currently a professor emeritus. A visiting
professor at the University of Erlangen, Germany; National Institute of Health,
Bethesda, MD, USA; Institute of Optics, Orsay, France; Institute Henri Poincaré,
Paris, France; International Centre for Signal Processing, Tampere University
of Technology, Finland; Agilent Laboratories, Palo Alto, CA, USA; Gunma
University, Kiryu, Japan; Autonomous University of Barcelona, Spain. Supervised
20 PhD candidates. An author and editor of more than 20 books and numerous
peer-reviewed publications on digital image processing and digital holography.

IOP Publishing

Advanced Digital Imaging Laboratory Using MATLAB®

Leonid P Yaroslavsky

Chapter 1

Introduction

1.1 General remarks about the book

This is an unusual book. It is a book of exercises, exercises in digital imaging engineering, one of the most important and rapidly developing branches of modern information technology. Studying digital imaging engineering, mastering this profession and working in the area is not possible without obtaining practical skills based on fundamental knowledge in the subject. The current book is aimed at providing technical support for this. It contains exercises on all major topics of digital imaging for students, researchers in experimental sciences and, generally, all practitioners in imaging engineering. It is based on the courses that have been taught by the author at Tel Aviv University and at a number of other universities in Europe and Japan during the last 15 years.

The key features of the book are the following.

1. The book supports studying and mastering of all fundamental aspects of digital imaging from image digitization to image resampling, recovery, parameter estimation, restoration and enhancement.
2. Exercises are designed and implemented in MATLAB®, which is commonly used in the electrical engineering community.
3. MATLAB® source codes for exercises are provided, which enable readers to modify them if necessary for particular needs, to design new exercises and, in addition, to use them for solving particular image processing tasks.
4. Exercises are supported by clear and intuitive explanations of the relevant theory.
5. Test signals and images provided in the book as well as the methodology of the experiments will be useful for readers in their further studies and practical work.

Altogether, the book contains 88 exercises that are grouped in eight chapters according to their subjects. They are listed in table 1.1.

doi:10.1088/978-0-750-31050-5ch1

Table 1.1. Nomenclature of exercises.

Chapter 2 Image digitization

Discretization

1   Energy compaction capability of transforms
2   Image band limitation
3   Estimating image effective bandwidth
4   Sampling artifacts: Strobe-effect
5   Sampling artifacts: Moire-effect
6   Ideal versus non-ideal sampling

Signal scalar quantization

7   Image 'scalar' quantization and 'false contours'
8   Vision sensitivity threshold
9   Quantization in a given range
10 Uniform versus Lloyd-Max quantization
11 Quantization with noise
12 Quantization of image spectra

Image data compression

13 Predictive coding: Prediction errors: 1D and 2D prediction
14 Predictive coding: DPCM coding: 1D versus 2D prediction
15 Transform coding

Chapter 3 Digital image formation and computational imaging

16 Image recovery from sparse samples
17 Recovery of images with occlusions

Numerical reconstruction of holograms

18 Reconstruction of a simulated Fresnel hologram
19 Reconstruction of a real off-axis hologram
20 Comparison of Fourier and Convolutional reconstruction algorithms
21 Image reconstruction from projections

Chapter 4 Image resampling and building continuous image models

Signal/image subsampling through fractional shifts

22 1D signal
23 2D image

Image resampling using 'continuous' image model

24 Extracting image arbitrary profiles
25 Image local zoom
26 Image resampling according to pixel X/Y displacement maps
27 Cartesian-to-polar coordinate conversion
28 Three step image rotation algorithm

Table 1.1. (*Continued.*)

(*Continues*)

Table 1.1. (*Continued.*)

Table 1.1. *(Continued.)*

Contrast enhancement: P**th** *law spectra enhancement*
81   Global spectrum enhancement
82   Local spectra enhancement

Contrast enhancement: P-histogram equalization
    83   Global *P*-histogram equalization
    84   Local *P*-histogram equalization

Contrast enhancement: pixel cardinalities
85   Global cardinalities
86   Local cardinalities

Contrast enhancement: edge extraction
87   Max–Min
88   Size-EV

The theoretical foundations of all methods represented by exercises in this book can be found in either of the following two books:

1. L Yaroslavsky, *Theoretical Foundations of Digital Imaging Using MATLAB®*, CRC Press, 2013.
2. L Yaroslavsky, *Digital Holography and Digital Image Processing*, Kluwer, 2004.

The reader should refer to these books for explanations, substantiations and derivations of the methods and algorithms implemented in the exercises.

1.2 Instructions for readers

To use the book and conduct exercises on a reader's computer, MATLAB® should be installed on the computer, the Advanced Digital Imaging Lab package that supplements the book should be copied into the computer and the MATLAB® path should be set to enable access to it from the MATLAB® command window. For some exercises, the availability of MATLAB® Signal Processing and Image Processing toolboxes is required. The package contains, in addition to program files, a set of test images in 'mat', 'tif' and 'jpg' formats. The usage for experimentation of images from users' image databases is also possible. The package was tested on MATLAB® R2010b version 7.11.0.584, but earlier versions can also be used.

The start program of the package is *Run_Labs_IOP*. The program opens the general entrance menu with a list of exercises shown in figure 1.1.

Items in this list unify sets of exercises on solving specific image processing tasks considered in the corresponding book chapter (see table 1.1). A particular set of exercises can be started by pressing the corresponding button in this menu.

The book chapters from 2 to 9 provide guidance for the exercises. The chapters explain the image processing task for which exercises of the particular chapter are

Figure 1.1. The general entrance menu.

designed; review basic principles underlying the corresponding methods; and give instructions for setting relevant parameters and running the exercises. It is recommended to read, before starting any particular set of exercises, the corresponding chapter.

It is also highly recommended to conduct the exercises with many different test images and with varieties of parameters of the algorithms in order to gain deeper insight into peculiarities of the algorithms and methods and their potentials and limitations, as well as how to properly set their user-defined working parameters.

At the end of each chapter, questions for self-testing are offered. They are intended to induce the reader to think over the results of the exercises and formulate for him/herself what has been learned.

The author wishes the readers a fascinating journey over the land of digital imaging and will appreciate any remarks, comments and program improvements.

IOP Publishing

Advanced Digital Imaging Laboratory Using MATLAB®

Leonid P Yaroslavsky

Chapter 2

Image digitization

2.1 Introduction

Exercises in this chapter address the very first problem of digital imaging, the problem of conversion of sensor signals that carry information on natural objects into digital signals that can be put into computers, stored in digital storage, transmitted through digital communication channels and eventually used for creating sufficiently perfect images. This conversion is called 'image digitization'.

Generally, image digitization can be treated as the determination, for each particular image, of which image in an indexed set of all possible images that the user can distinguish from one another, can be identified with that particular image. The index of this 'representative' image in the set is taken as the image digital representation. Image reconstruction from its digital representation then generates the representative image with this index. This is similar, for instance, to what we do when we describe everything in our life with words in speaking or writing.

However, in the case of images, this general procedure is, as a rule, not feasible in reality. While the volume of our vocabulary is about 10^5–10^6 words, the variety of images we have to deal with in imaging is immeasurably larger. One can see this from a simple example: the number of digital images of, for instance, standard (not high-definition) TV quality (500 × 500 *pixels* with 256 gray levels in each of three RGB channels) is $256^{3\times500\times500}$. One can hardly imagine a technical device capable of implementing such a huge look-up table, as this number overwhelmingly exceeds the number of elementary particles in the Universe.

A solution of this problem of image digitization complexity is found in a three-stage digitization procedure. In the first stage, called *image discretization*, continuous sensor signals are converted into a finite set of real numbers that form the *image discrete representation*.

In the second stage, called *scalar (element wise) quantization*, this set of real numbers is, number by number, converted into a set of quantized numbers, which finally results in a digital signal that can be used for reconstruction, with a certain admissible accuracy, of the initial continuous signal. In the same way as written speech is a sequence of letters selected from an alphabet, digital representation of images is a sequence of numbers that can take one of a finite set of quantized values.

In the third stage, called *image compression*, digital signals obtained after discretization and scalar quantization are subjected to 'compression' aimed at minimization of the number of binary digits (bits) sufficient to represent them and, hence, at minimization of the size of the memory required for storing images in digital storage or of the capacity of digital communication channels used for image transmission.

To study these issues, the following three corresponding sets of laboratory exercises are offered.

- Image digitization: discretization.
- Image digitization: scalar quantization.
- Image digitization: image data compression.

2.2 Image discretization

Upon pressing the button 'Image digitization: discretization' in the main menu of exercises, the panel shown in figure 2.1 appears, which offers two groups of exercises.

The first two exercises, 'Energy compaction capability of transforms' and 'Image band limitation', illustrate the basic principle of discretization as image expansion over a set of transform basis functions. The last three exercises, 'Estimating image effective bandwidth', 'Sampling artifacts', and 'Ideal versus non-ideal sampling' aim

Figure 2.1. List of exercises in the section 'Image digitization: discretization'.

to assist the study of the most commonly used image discretization method, that of image sampling.

2.2.1 Signal discretization as expansion over a set of basis functions

In principle, there might be many different ways to convert continuous image sensor signals into discrete ones represented by sets of real numbers. However, the technological tradition is such that technical devices used currently for such a conversion implement a method that can mathematically be modeled as computing coefficients of image signal expansion (decomposition) over a set of basis functions of a certain transform, i.e. over a set of transform template images.

The coefficients $\{\alpha_{k,l}\}$ of signal discrete representations with $\{k, l\}$ as coefficient integer indices are computed in image discretization devices as

$$\alpha_{k,l} = \int_X \int_Y a(x, y)\varphi_{k,l}^{(d)}(x, y) \, dx \, dy \tag{2.1}$$

where $\varphi_{k,l}^{(d)}(x, y)$ are basis functions defined in the image discretization device coordinate system (x, y) and used for image discretization. Functions $\varphi_{k,l}^{(d)}(x, y)$ describe the spatial sensitivity of image discretization devices, i.e. their *point spread function*.

Image discretization with discretization basis $\{\varphi_{k,l}^{(d)}(x, y)\}$ assumes that a reciprocal set of reconstructing basis functions $\{\varphi_{k,l}^{(r)}(x, y)\}$ exists, with which the image $a(x, y)$ can be reconstructed from its discrete representation coefficients $\{\alpha_{k,l}\}$ as the following:

$$a(x, y) \approx \sum_{k=0}^{K-1} \sum_{l=0}^{L-1} \alpha_{k,l}\varphi_{k,l}^{(r)}(x, y) \tag{2.2}$$

where the approximation symbol $\approx$ indicates that images reconstructed from its discrete representation $\{\alpha_{k,l}\}$ are, generally, not precise copies of the initial images, $K \times L$ is the number of representation coefficients needed for image reconstruction with a desired accuracy and functions $\{\varphi_{k,l}^{(r)}(x, y)\}$ are point spread functions of signal reconstruction devices (such as, for instance, computer displays), or their *reconstruction aperture functions*.

For different bases, the signal approximation accuracy for a given number of basis functions $N = K \times L$ used for image reconstruction might be different. Naturally, the discretization and reconstruction bases that provide better approximation accuracy for a given N are preferable. It is customary to evaluate the signal approximation accuracy in terms of preservation of *signal energy*, i.e. of the integral of the squared signal over its definition area. The capability of transforms to concentrate signal energy in a few signal decomposition coefficients is called their *energy compaction capability*.

Theoretically, the Karhunen–Loève transform and the related Hotelling and singular value decomposition (SVD) transforms have the best energy compaction capability among discretization transforms. However, in practice in image processing they remain, because of implementation problems, to serve only as theoretical benchmarks, and other transforms that have fast computational algorithms, such as discrete Fourier (DFT), discrete cosine (DCT), discrete Walsh and discrete Haar transforms, are used as discretization and, correspondingly, reconstruction transforms.

The exercise 'Energy compaction capability of transforms' offers an opportunity to compare the energy compaction capability of these transforms in application to different test images. In this exercise, spectra of images in different transforms are computed and spectral coefficients are sorted according to their magnitude. Then a certain percentage of the coefficients with the least magnitudes is zeroed, after which such 'band-limited' images are reconstructed and displayed along with their 'band-limited' spectra to enable their visual comparison. In addition, fractions of image energy contained in the retained coefficients are computed and plotted as functions of the percentage of retained transform coefficients. The latter is a numerical measure of the transform energy compaction capability (see an example in figure 2.2).

The exercise can be conducted either with image frames of 256×256 pixels or with interactively selected image fragments of different size.

An alternative insight into the energy compaction capability of transforms provides the second exercise of this group, 'Image band limitation'. In this experiment, image reconstruction quality is compared, when images are subjected to 'low-pass' filtering, i.e. when only spectral coefficients with sufficiently low indices are retained and the rest are zeroed. In the case of discrete Fourier and discrete cosine transforms, spectral coefficients that correspond to sufficiently low image spatial frequencies are retained. The exercise allows us (i) to examine how the energy of spectral coefficients depends on the spectrum 'low-pass' band limitation by a square or

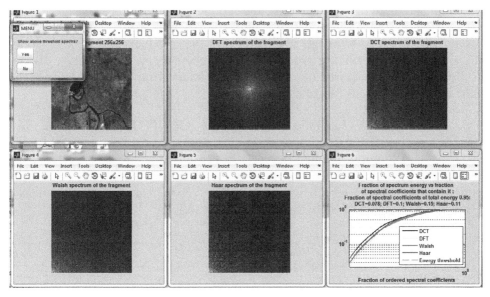

Figure 2.2. An example of displays generated when running the exercise 'Energy compaction capability of transforms'.

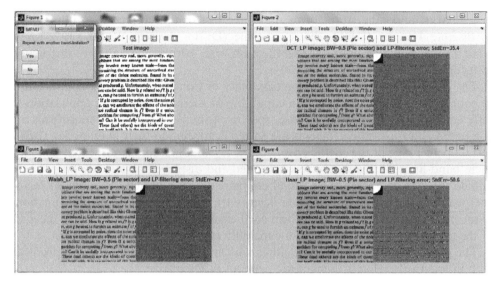

Figure 2.3. An example of displays generated when running the exercise 'Image band limitation' (band limitation by a pie sector).

a pie sector, and (ii) to visually evaluate results of image band limitation for different transforms and to compare standard deviations of reconstruction errors due to spectrum band limitation. Figure 2.3 illustrates how results of this exercise are displayed.

2.2.2 Image sampling

Among image discretization methods, the representation of images in the form of arrays of samples taken in nodes of a uniform rectangular sampling lattice is the most commonly used. Although imaging devices that produce images may work on different principles, for image processing software and especially for image displays such representation is the standard. In sampling, image samples are measured using 'shift', or sampling basis functions as

$$\alpha_{k,l} = \int_X \int_Y a(x, y)\varphi^{(s)}\left(x - k\Delta^{(s)}x, y - l\Delta^{(s)}y\right) dx\, dy \tag{2.3}$$

where $(\Delta^{(s)}x, \Delta^{(s)}y)$ are sampling intervals in two coordinates and $\varphi^{(s)}(x, y)$ is the point spread function (*sampling aperture*) of the sampling device, such as an image scanner, digital camera or similar. Correspondingly, image reconstruction in display devices is performed with shift basis functions as well:

$$a(x, y) \approx \sum_{k=0}^{K-1} \sum_{l=0}^{L-1} \alpha_{k,l}\varphi^{(r)}\left(x - k\Delta^{(r)}x, y - l\Delta^{(r)}y\right) \tag{2.4}$$

where $\Delta^{(r)}x$ and $\Delta^{(r)}y$ are corresponding sampling intervals over (x, y) coordinates of the image reconstruction device and $\varphi^{(r)}(x, y)$ is the image reconstruction device point spread function (*reconstruction aperture*).

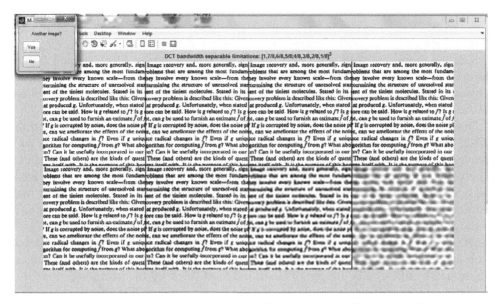

Figure 2.4. A sample display of the exercise 'Estimating image effective bandwidth'.

Sampling intervals $\Delta^{(s)}x$ and $\Delta^{(s)}y$ define the dimensions ($1/\Delta^{(s)}x$, $1/\Delta^{(s)}y$) of the image *baseband* in the domain of the image Fourier transform. In order to reduce computer memory and image processing time, they should be selected as large as possible but not larger than allowed by the requirements for image 'readability'. The exercise 'Estimating image effective bandwidth' offers an opportunity to visually evaluate how the selection of image basebands and, correspondingly, of image sampling intervals affects the 'readability' of different images. Examples of images with different band limitations generated in the exercise are shown in figure 2.4.

The theoretical foundation of image sampling is provided by *sampling theory*. Image sampling inevitably causes certain image distortions. According to sampling theory, these distortions in the reconstructed images are due to the following factors:

- modification of the image Fourier spectra due to image pre-filtering in sampling devices;
- penetration of tails of the pre-filtered image spectrum periodical (with periods ($1/\Delta^{(s)}x$, $1/\Delta^{(s)}y$)) replicas inside the image baseband, which causes spectrum *aliasing*;
- penetration into spectra of reconstructed images of the image spectrum periodical replicas outside the signal baseband, which are not perfectly filtered out by 'post-filtering' in the image reconstruction device.

Sampling theory states that these distortions are minimal if sampling and reconstruction apertures are sinc functions $\text{sinc}(x) = (\sin x)/x$:

$$\varphi_{k,l}^{(s)}(x, y) = \left(1/\Delta^{(s)}x\Delta^{(s)}y\right)\text{sinc}\left[\pi\left(x - k\Delta^{(s)}x\right)/\Delta^{(s)}x\right]\text{sinc}\left[\pi\left(y - k\Delta^{(s)}y\right)/\Delta^{(s)}y\right] \quad (2.5)$$

$$\varphi_{k,l}^{(r)}(x, y) = \mathrm{sinc}\left[\pi\left(x - k\Delta^{(r)}x\right)/\Delta^{(r)}x\right]\mathrm{sinc}\left[\pi\left(y - k\Delta^{(r)}y\right)/\Delta^{(r)}y\right]. \qquad (2.6)$$

Sinc functions are point spread functions of ideal low-pass filters, which do not distort image spectra within the baseband and remove all spectral components outside the baseband, thus preventing image spectra from aliasing due to sampling. Image pre-filtering with the ideal low-pass filter makes images band limited.

One of the most characteristic and clearly visible sampling artifacts is the *strobe effect*, i.e. stroboscopic reduction of frequency of periodical signal components with frequencies that exceed the highest frequencies ($1/2\Delta^{(s)}x$, $1/2\Delta^{(s)}y$) of the signal baseband. If the signal is properly pre-filtered, such components are removed from the signal. Otherwise, their replicated copies will enter the baseband and appear with reduced frequencies. Specifically, a component with frequency $f_x > 1/2\Delta^{(s)}x$ appears in the reconstructed signal with frequency ($1/\Delta^{(s)}x - f_x$).

Another sampling artifact characteristic of periodical signals is the *moiré effect*. It is observed when the reconstruction of signals from their samples is made with filters whose passband exceeds the signal baseband as defined by the sampling interval.

These sampling artifacts are demonstrated in the exercise 'Sampling artifacts' on examples of sinusoidal test signals of different frequencies. Figures 2.5 and 2.6 show examples of illustrative plots generated in this exercise.

Appropriate pre- and post-filtering for image sampling may have a profound positive effect on performing image analysis tasks. The exercise 'Ideal versus non-ideal sampling' is intended for the comparison of 'ideal' and 'non-ideal' samplings of different test images. An example of outputs of this exercise is shown in figure 2.7.

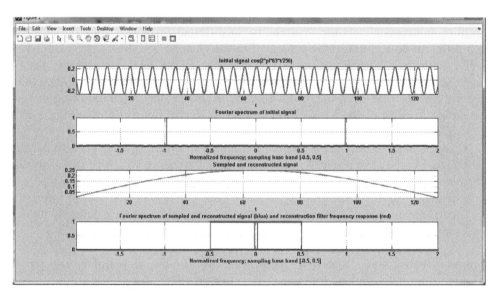

Figure 2.5. Illustration of the 'strobe' effect in sampling and reconstruction of an inappropriately pre-filtered sinusoidal signal, whose frequency exceeds the highest frequency of the signal baseband.

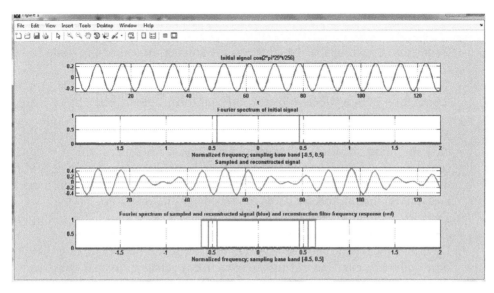

Figure 2.6. Moiré effect in sampling and reconstruction of a sinusoidal signal in the case of inappropriate 'post-filtering'.

Figure 2.7. Image sampling with ideal versus non-ideal pre- and post-filtering.

2.2.3 Questions for self-testing

1. From your experiments, how would you rate, on average, DFT, DCT, Walsh and Haar transforms in terms of their energy compaction capability?
2. When is the energy compaction capability of a transform more pronounced, for image frames or for image fragments?

3. As a rule, the Haar transform has lower energy compaction capability than DCT, DFT and Walsh transforms. However, for some images and image fragments it exhibits a better energy compaction capability than other transforms. Can you associate this fact with the type of image?

4. Were your estimations of admissible image band limitations in the exercise 'Estimating image effective bandwidth' uniform over all the sets of images you tested?

5. Suppose you have an image to scan or a scene to be photographed and you have an image scanner with a certain resolution (dots per inch) or a digital camera with a certain number of pixels per frame. How would you determine whether these devices are sufficient for doing the job? Would you need to measure the image spectra to be able to make the decision?

6. Describe as many sampling artifacts observed in the exercise 'Sampling artifacts' as you can.

7. Describe and explain the distortions in images due to undersampling that you observed while carrying out the exercise 'Ideal versus non-ideal sampling'.

2.3 Signal scalar quantization

2.3.1 Exercises

Scalar (element-wise) quantization is the second stage of image digitization. It is applied to image discrete representation coefficients obtained as a result of image discretization. Scalar quantization implies that a finite interval has first to be specified in the entire range of magnitude of the image representation coefficient values $\{\alpha\}$ by defining their minimum α_{min} and maximum α_{max}, and then the interval $[\alpha_{min}, \alpha_{max}]$ is split into a certain number Q of *quantization intervals* by defining their border values $\{\alpha^{(q)}\}$, $q = 0, 1,..., Q-1$. Quantization intervals are indexed by an integer index and for each particular qth interval the representative value, or *quantization level* $\aleph^{(q)}$, is chosen. For image reconstruction, all values within a particular quantization interval are replaced with its representative quantization level.

The difference $\varepsilon^{(q)} = \alpha - \aleph^{(q)}$ between the true value α and its corresponding quantization level $\aleph^{(q)}$ is called the *quantization error*. Quantization errors within the dynamic range are limited in the range by the size of the quantization intervals, whereas dynamic range limitation errors may, in principle, be unlimited in value.

The arrangement of quantization intervals and selection of quantization levels are governed by requirements on the accuracy of the image quantized representation, which are generally formulated in terms of certain constraints imposed on quantization errors. With the most common approach to formulating the constraints, losses due to quantization errors are evaluated on average over all possible coefficient values.

There are two approaches to the design of optimal quantizers, a direct optimization approach and a *compressor–expander (compander)* one. The direct optimization approach assumes numerical optimization of quantization interval borders and representative quantization levels for an image database, for a certain statistical model of image representation coefficients or for particular image frames.

Compressor–expander quantization is a simplified method of optimal non-uniform quantization. With this method, the signal is subjected to a certain nonlinear point-wise transformation and after that is uniformly quantized. Correspondingly, at the reconstruction stage, uniformly quantized values have to be subjected to a nonlinear transformation inverse to the one used for quantization.

Usually, the required nonlinear pre-quantization transformation compresses the signal dynamic range, hence the name 'compressor–expander quantization'. Optimization of the compressor–expander quantization is achieved by an appropriate selection of the compressive nonlinear pointwise transformation.

In quantization of image sample (pixel) gray levels, artifacts of quantization exhibit themselves most frequently in the appearance of visible boundaries between image patches quantized to different quantization levels. They are called *false contours*. The exercise 'Image scalar quantization and "false contours"' is designed for studying this phenomenon for different test images and different numbers of quantization levels. An example of its outcomes is presented in figure 2.8.

A natural primary requirement for quantization of image gray levels is to secure the invisibility of false contours in displayed digital images. The visibility of patches of constant gray level depends on their contrast with respect to their background and on the size of the patches. Using the exercise 'Vision sensitivity threshold' one can determine one's own visual sensitivity threshold. In the exercise, a square stimulus of certain contrast is displayed in a random position within the field of view on an empty background, and the viewer is prompted to confirm whether he/she has detected the stimulus.

The experiment begins with a stimulus of the smallest size of one pixel and of the lower contrast of one gray level, assuming a total of 255 gray levels of image dynamic range. If the stimulus is not detected, its contrast is raised by one

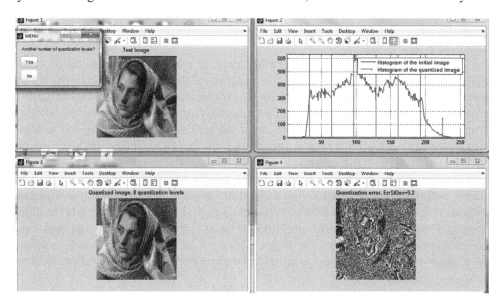

Figure 2.8. False contours in quantization of image pixel gray levels.

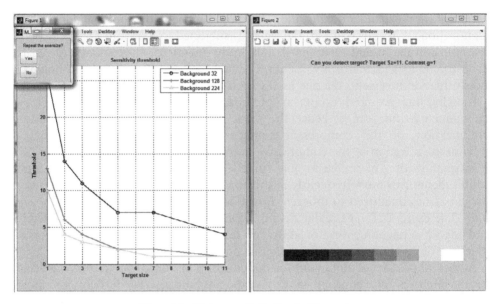

Figure 2.9. 'Vision sensitivity threshold' exercise.

quantization level and the experiment is repeated until the stimulus is detected. The reached contrast is saved as the threshold visibility contrast for this stimulus size, and then a new series of tests begins with stimuli of larger size (3 × 3, 5 × 5, 7 × 7 and 11 × 11 pixels). After testing the stimulus of the largest size, the same is repeated for another gray level of the background. A total of three background gray levels are tested: one in the middle of the image dynamic range (gray level 128), one in the lower half (gray level 32) and one in the upper half (gray level 224) of the displayed image dynamic range 0–255. Figure 2.9 is an example of visualizing the results of this exercise.

The exercise 'Quantization in a given range' is intended for training in image scalar quantization and specifically for experimentation in selecting limits of the image dynamic range and of the number of quantization levels. The quantization range of images is specified in terms of its ratio to image standard deviation, and it is symmetrical with respect to the image mean value. The viewer is prompted to select this ratio for the chosen test image, specify the number of quantization levels within the selected dynamic range and visually evaluate the quality of the displayed quantized image. An example of outcomes of this exercise is presented in figure 2.10.

The uniform arrangement of quantization levels is the simplest quantization method. It is usually implemented in analog-to-digital convertors of digital imaging devices. However, as already mentioned, it is, in general, not optimal, and quantization errors might be, for a given number of quantization levels, reduced using an appropriately selected non-uniform arrangement of quantization levels in the quantization range.

A direct quantization optimization method that minimizes, by means of a non-uniform arrangement of quantization levels, the standard deviation of quantization

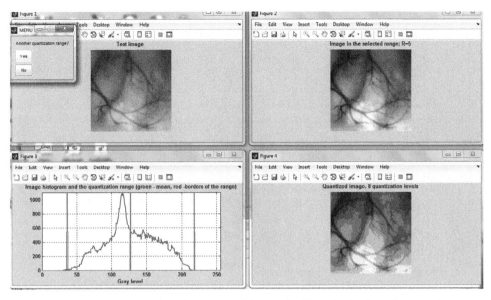

Figure 2.10. An illustration of outcomes of the exercise 'Quantization in a given range'.

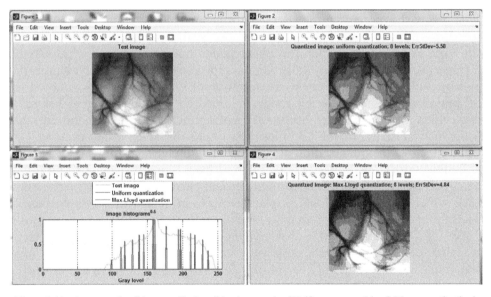

Figure 2.11. An example of images displayed in the exercise 'Uniform versus Lloyd-Max quantization'.

errors is called *Lloyd-Max quantization*. The exercise 'Uniform versus Lloyd-Max quantization' enables experimental comparison of the uniform and Lloyd-Max quantization in terms of the quantization error standard deviation for a given (by the user) number of image quantization levels and for different test images, both pre-prepared and selected by the user from his/her image database. Figure 2.11 illustrates results displayed in this exercise.

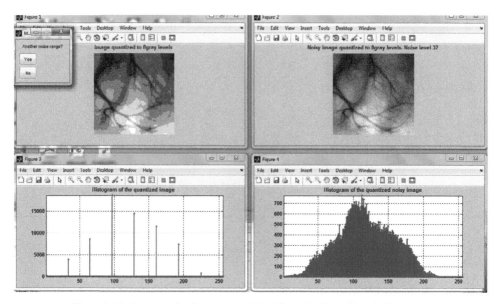

Figure 2.12. An example of outcomes of the 'Quantization with noise' exercise.

The visibility of false contours in the quantized image is dependent on noise, which might be present in image signals generated by image sensors. Noise randomizes false contours and makes them less visible. The exercise 'Quantization with noise' is intended to study this phenomenon and to determine what minimal noise level is sufficient to make false contours for a selected number of quantization levels invisible. In this experiment, a realization of random numbers with uniform distribution in the user-selected range is added to the image signal before its quantization, and the same realization is then subtracted from the quantized signal for the image display. Figure 2.12 illustrates results displayed in this exercise.

The effects of the quantization of coefficients of image transforms such as DFT, DCT and Walsh transforms are very different from those of quantizing pixel gray levels. Because each image transform coefficient carries information on the entire image rather than on individual pixels, quantization of the transform coefficients affects the entire image and produces a kind of spotty noise. The distribution density of transform coefficients within their dynamic range, which is substantially larger than that of pixel gray levels, is very non-uniform: coefficients with larger magnitudes, which are usually responsible for 'low-frequency' image components, are much rarer than 'high-frequency' coefficients with low magnitudes that carry information on object edges. Therefore, non-uniform compressive quantization is highly advisable for the quantization of image transform coefficients.

Improvements in the quality of reconstructed images achieved with the use of non-uniform quantization, implemented in the form of the so-called *Pth law* *'compander/expander' quantization* can be observed in the exercise 'Quantization of image spectra'. In *P*th law quantization, magnitudes of image transform coefficients are raised to a power $P < 1$ and are then uniformly quantized to a selected number of quantization levels in the range between zero and the maximal

Figure 2.13. Exercise 'Quantization of image spectra'. Results of optimization of parameter P of Pth law quantization are displayed along with images reconstructed for optimal P and for uniform quantization ($P = 1$).

value of the modified coefficients. For image reconstruction, quantized coefficients are raised to the inverse power $1/P$.

In the exercise, the quantization parameter P is optimized to minimize the standard deviation of image quantization errors. Note that in this case the total number of coefficient quantization levels is an odd number; for instance, for 33 quantization levels 16 levels are allocated for positive and 16 levels for negative values and one level is a 'zero' level. Figure 2.13 shows an example of the displayed results.

2.3.2 Questions for self-testing

1. In which image areas are false contours most annoying and in which are they least annoying and visible?
2. Is your vision sensitivity threshold the same for stimuli of all sizes and for all background levels?
3. Why are 256 gray levels selected as a standard for image quantized representation?
4. What would be your recommendation regarding selection of the pixel gray level quantization range?
5. Is uniform quantization optimal for the quantization of image gray levels?
6. Does Lloyd-Max quantization always substantially reduce quantization artifacts? Does it improve the image visual quality?
7. What would be your recommendation regarding selecting the intensity of additive noise that would be sufficient to hide quantization false contours?
8. From your experiments, do you think that there is a value of the parameter P for Pth law quantization of image transform coefficients that would be sufficiently appropriate for the majority of images?

2.4 Image compression

2.4.1 Exercises

As mentioned, image representation in the form of arrays of samples taken at nodes of uniform rectangular sampling lattices is the most frequently used method of image discretization. It is also standard for image displays, which means that any imaging system and image processing should ultimately produce sampled images for display. However, the sampled representation of images is as a rule very redundant in terms of the volume of data needed to produce images of admissible quality. The reason is that image samples should be taken densely enough to secure a good reproduction of object edges, though edges usually occupy only a small fraction of the image area. This redundancy amounts to tens and, for some images, even hundreds of times. The same refers to video data represented as sets of video frames, which are also highly redundant. In addition to this, scalar quantization of pixel gray levels also requires an excessive number of quantization levels in order to secure invisibility of quantization artifacts, such as false contours, to which the most vulnerable are exactly those excessive image samples from non-edgy image areas.

All this means that, for image data storage and transmission, sampled image representation can be substantially compressed. The compression is usually conducted as a supplemental image processing applied to the 'primary' sampled image representation.

Basically, there are two groups of image compression methods: predictive and transform.

In *predictive compression methods*, pixel-wise differences between the pixel gray level and its predicted estimate found as a weighted sum over pixels that surround the given one on the sampling lattice are computed and then subjected to scalar quantization. The method, in which the 'prediction' and computing differences is performed in the course of image row-wise/column-wise scanning, is called *differential pulse code modulation (DPCM)*. In DPCM, a difference between the current pixel gray level and its value predicted from previously scanned neighboring pixels is quantized and then encoded for transmission or storage. In 1D DPCM, the predicted value is the gray level of the pixel preceding the given one on the scanning row weighted by the correlation coefficient between two adjacent pixels. In 2D DPCM, the weighted average over pixels nearest to the given one in the previous scanning row and the previous pixel in the given row is used as a predicted value. DPCM is historically the earliest data compression method. Nowadays it is used solely for 'interframe' coding of video sequences; however, the method is very instructive for understanding basic principles of data compression.

In *transform image compression*, it is the image transform coefficients that undergo scalar quantization. In principle, transform compression can be applied image frame-wise or block-wise. In frame-wise compression, the image frame as a whole is transformed, transform coefficients with sufficiently low energy are truncated and the remaining ones are quantized using the optimal non-uniform quantization. In block-wise compression, the image is split into non-overlapping blocks of relatively small size and transforms are applied to individual blocks separately. For every block, low-energy block transform coefficients are truncated and the remaining ones are optimally quantized.

Applying transforms block-wise is well suited to image spatial inhomogeneity, and transform coefficient quantization can be better optimized if it is performed individually for transform spectra of image blocks. The size of blocks is determined by the degree of image inhomogeneity and, in principle, can vary within an image frame: it should be as large as possible provided the image remains 'homogeneous' within the block. Among block transforms, DCT proved to be the best one and it is put as the basis of modern image and video compression standards JPEG and MPEG.

The set of exercises 'Image compression' is intended for experimentation in predictive and transform image compression. 1D and 2D DPCM and block-wise transform coding in the DCT domain are implemented.

In the section 'Predictive coding' one can evaluate and compare distribution histograms and standard deviations of prediction errors in the case of 1D and 2D prediction for different images. They are key parameters for the optimization of prediction error quantization. An example of results obtained in this exercise is shown in figure 2.14.

In the section 'DPCM coding: 1D versus 2D prediction', DPCM with 1D and 2D predictions is implemented for comparison of prediction efficiency for different images and evaluation of immunity to impulse noise in communication channels. Parameters of the exercise are the dynamic range of the quantized prediction error and the probability of error in transmission of the quantized prediction error. In this implementation, the Pth law quantization of magnitudes of prediction errors is used and the optimal value of the parameter P, which minimizes the mean square image

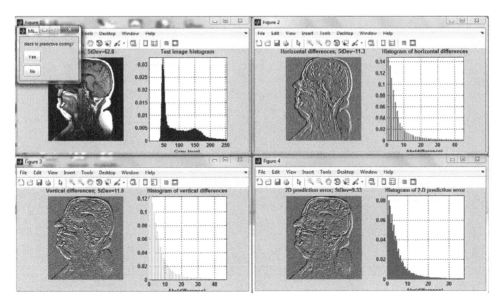

Figure 2.14. An example of output displays in the exercise 'Prediction errors: 1D and 2D prediction'.

reconstruction error, is found for each particular test image selected by the user. Figure 2.15 presents a sample of displayed results of this exercise.

In the section 'Transform coding', the block-wise DCT domain image compression method is implemented to evaluate its efficiency in terms of the number of bits per pixel and the mean square image reconstruction error. Parameters of the exercise are the size of blocks (in pixels), the fraction of transform coefficients left for

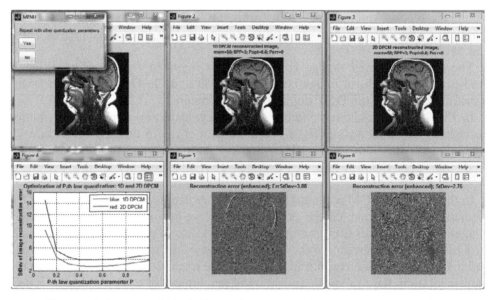

Figure 2.15. An output display in the exercise 'DPCM coding: 1D versus 2D prediction'.

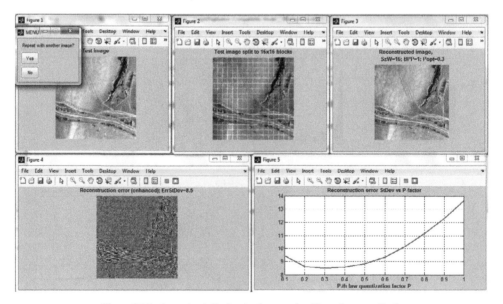

Figure 2.16. An output display in the exercise 'Transform coding'.

quantization and the number of their quantization levels. Truncation of DCT spectral coefficients of image blocks is implemented by means of zeroing coefficients outside of a spectral mask in the form of a pie sector whose area is a fraction of the block area selected by the user. Nonlinear quantization of retained coefficients is implemented as the Pth law quantization with parameter P optimized for each particular image. An example of displayed results is presented in figure 2.16.

2.4.2 Questions for self-testing

1. How would you formulate the basic principle of image data compression?
2. Why and when is image compression possible?
3. What is your estimate of how much lower the standard deviation of DPCM prediction errors is than that of the corresponding images, and how much one can expect to gain in terms of the required number of quantization levels?
4. Is 2D DPCM substantially more efficient in terms of image data compression than 1D DPCM?
5. Are 1D and 2D DPCM equally vulnerable to communication channel noise?
6. What is the main difference between the effects of communication channel noise in 1D DPCM and 2D DPCM?
7. What would be your recommendation regarding selecting the block size for DCT transform coding for a given particular image?
8. What artifacts are characteristic for block transform compression?
9. What factor is more decisive for compression efficiency: the number of transform coefficient quantization levels or the fraction of transform coefficients retained for quantization?

Chapter 3

Digital image formation and computational imaging

3.1 Introduction

This chapter is devoted to computational image formation from numerical data, or computational imaging. Apparently, the earliest examples of computational imaging are computed tomography and digital holography. In computed tomography discrete numerical data of object slice projections obtained under a set of angles are converted into a set of samples of slice images over a regular square sampling grid suited for conventional image displays. In digital holography, samples of electronically recorded optical or other types of hologram of real objects are used for the numerical reconstruction of images of the objects. Nowadays, thanks to remarkable progress in computer power and capacity, computational imaging is used for solving imaging problems in many new areas where imaging was regarded as not feasible not long ago.

The set of exercises unified by the title 'Digital image formation and computational imaging' includes exercises in

- image recovery from sparse and irregular samples;
- recovery of images with occlusions;
- numerical reconstruction of holograms;
- image reconstruction from projections.

A pop-up menu for selecting exercises from this list is shown in figure 3.1.

3.2 Image recovery from sparse irregularly sampled data. Recovery of images with occlusions

There are many applications where, contrary to the common practice of uniform sampling, sampled data are collected in an irregular fashion. Here are some typical instances.

Figure 3.1. Digital image formation and computational imaging: a pop-up menu for selecting exercises.

1. Samples are taken not where the regular sampling grid dictates to take them but where it is feasible because of technical or other limitations.
2. The pattern of sample disposition is dictated by the physical principles of the working of the measuring device (as, for example, in interferometry or the moiré technique, where samples are taken along level lines).
3. Sampling device positioning is jittering due to camera or object vibrations or due to other irregularities as in imaging through a turbulent medium.
4. Some samples of the regular sampling grid are lost or unavailable due to losses in communication channels or other factors. It also frequently happens that missing samples form spatial clusters, which cause image occlusions.

In all such cases, recovery of all image samples from those available is required. Obviously, this is not possible without bringing in *a priori* knowledge regarding the images to be recovered and defining a method for the evaluation of the fidelity of the recovery.

In the assumption that image recovery is evaluated in terms of a mean square recovery error, an attractive framework for solving this problem is provided by the *discrete sampling theorem*. The discrete sampling theorem states that if K of N required samples of signals ($K < N$) are available the signals can be approximated by their band-limited, in a certain selected transform domain, copies with a mean square approximation error equal to the energy of their $N - K$ neglected (i.e. zeroed) transform coefficients; the approximation error can be minimized by means of band limitation in a domain of transform with the best, for the particular class of signals, energy compaction capability. The type of the transform and the degree of band limitation are the *a priori* knowledge that one brings in to solve the problem of signal recovery from sparse samples. In a special case of band-limited (in a certain transform) signals, precise recovery is possible.

In principle, such an approximation of images requires inversing of very large matrices, which is in many cases not feasible. Another option is using an iterative algorithm that works alternately in the image and transform domains by means of introducing constraints: available pixels in their known positions in the image domain and the selected type of band limitation in the transform domain. A few hundred such iterations are usually sufficient for obtaining quite good band-limited image approximations.

The exercises 'Image recovery from sparse samples' and 'Recovery of images with occlusions' are implemented using the iterative algorithm and provide an opportunity to gain a practical insight into the capability of iterative image reconstruction from sparse samples and filling in occlusions. Several test images are pre-prepared for these exercises. Working with arbitrary images from the user image database is also possible.

Among pre-prepared test images, there is a 'band-limited and space-limited' image, which, according to the discrete sampling theorem, can be precisely recovered if the number of its available pixels is equal to or larger than the number of non-zero coefficients of its spectrum. This test image was generated using iterative image filtering alternately in the transform domain and the image domain, imposing a band limitation in the transform domain and a space limitation in the image domain.

As a transform, DCT is selected, and band limitation of signals is implemented as limitation by a binary mask in the form of a 'pie sector' with a radius that corresponds to the given fraction of the total number of image DCT coefficients.

To run the exercise 'Image recovery from sparse samples', the user is prompted to select the test image, the number of randomly placed image samples (in fractions of the image size) and the number of iterations. The number of image samples is used to automatically determine the radius of the pie-sector binary mask for image band limitation in the DCT domain. An exemplary result of running the 'Image recovery from sparse or non-uniformly sampled data' exercise is presented in figure 3.2.

In the exercise 'Recovery of images with occlusions', image occlusions are imitated in the form of stripes with lengths of 3 or 5 pixels and of 3×3 or 5×5 pixel squares. The user is prompted to select a test image, the number of iterations and rate of occlusions (as a fraction of the number of test image pixels) and the type of occlusion. The rate of occlusions is used to determine the radius of the pie-sector binary mask for image band limitation according to the discrete sampling theorem.

In order to speed up the iterative image reconstruction it is advisable to introduce a certain redundancy to the number of available pixels with respect to the number of image non-zero spectral coefficients (the area of the pie-sector band-limiting mask). The recommended redundancy is of the order of the ratio $4/\pi$ of the area of a square to the area of a pie sector inscribed into this square. Figure 3.3 exemplifies how the results of the exercise are presented.

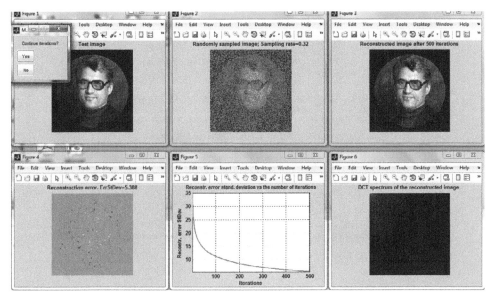

Figure 3.2. An example of a run of the exercise 'Image recovery from sparse or non-uniformly sampled data'.

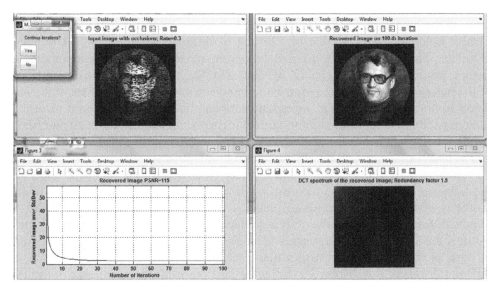

Figure 3.3. An example of a run of the exercise 'Recovery of images with occlusions'.

3.3 Numerical reconstruction of holograms

Three exercises are offered in this section (figure 3.4):
- reconstruction of a simulated Fresnel hologram
- reconstruction of a real off-axis hologram
- comparison of Fourier and convolutional reconstruction algorithms.

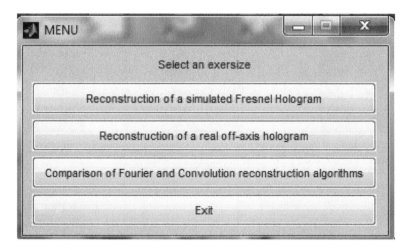

Figure 3.4. List of exercises 'Numerical reconstruction of holograms'.

Holograms are recorded amplitudes and phases of radiation wavefronts emitted by physical objects. Fresnel holograms are holograms recorded in the so-called 'near diffraction zone', where the wavefront phase shift component proportional to the ratio of the hologram size to the object-to-hologram distance cannot be neglected. Fresnel holograms are capable of focusing to different object planes at different distances. The algorithm for Fresnel hologram reconstruction contains a dimensionless distance parameter $\mu^2 = \lambda Z/\Delta f^2 N = \lambda Z/\Delta f S z_h$, that links physical parameters of the holograms and the hologram sampling device: wavelength λ of the radiation, object-to-hologram distance Z, hologram sampling interval Δf (hologram recording camera pitch), number of hologram samples N (in one dimension; the total number of a square hologram is N^2) and the physical 1D dimension of the hologram $S z_h = \Delta f N$.

The exercise 'Numerical reconstruction of holograms' simulates the formation of a Fresnel hologram of four test pictures placed at different positions with respect to the hologram plane and the reconstruction of images from the hologram. In the synthesis of holograms, a random phase is assigned to test pictures in order to imitate diffuse properties of the objects' surfaces. Position parameters (μ^2) of the test pictures are user-defined parameters. The program computes a Fresnel hologram of these pictures and demonstrates their reconstruction by means of 'focusing' at different distances and displaying the reconstruction results as a sequence of frames. One of the displays is shown in figure 3.5.

Two other exercises demonstrate the reconstruction of real, not simulated, holograms. As physical radiation sensors are sensitive to only the intensity of radiation, for recording optical holograms the hologram recording sensor is illuminated by an 'object' light beam reflected from the object or passed through it and by a reference light beam. The two beams form a sinusoidal interference pattern modulated by the amplitude and phase of the object wavefront.

Two complementing methods of hologram recording are used: 'off-axis' and 'on-axis' recording methods. In the 'off-axis' method, the reference beam is

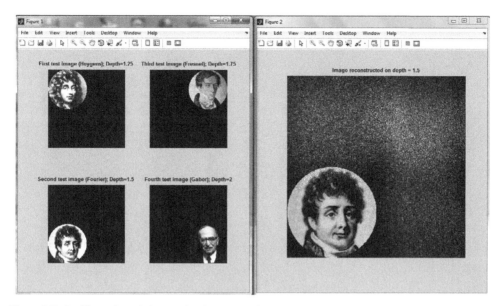

Figure 3.5. An illustration of the exercise 'Reconstruction of simulated Fresnel hologram' (left, test images placed at different distances from the hologram; right, a result of reconstruction of one of the images).

directed onto the hologram at a certain angle with respect to the object beam, sufficiently large to enable separation of real and imaginary images, which are reconstructed from the sinusoidal interference pattern. In this case, applying the 'backpropagation' transform directly to the recorded hologram is sufficient for hologram reconstruction.

While the 'off-axis' method is suitable for both optical and numerical reconstruction of holograms, the 'on-axis' method is suitable only for numerical reconstruction. In the 'on-axis' method, the reference beam is collinear with the object beam. If the 'backpropagation' transform is applied to the recorded hologram in this way, real and imaginary object images overlay each other in the reconstructed image. In order to avoid this overlay, one needs to be able to separate amplitude and phase components in the recorded hologram. To enable this, 'on-axis' holograms are recorded in several exposures (usually three or four) with appropriate changes of the reference beam phase. The amplitude and phase components of the recorded wavefront are then numerically separated from these recordings.

In the exercise 'Reconstruction of a real off-axis hologram', the program carries out reconstruction of a real optical Fresnel hologram of a die for different hologram-to-object distances and displays the reconstruction results as illustrated in figure 3.6.

Reconstruction of a real 'on-axis' hologram is demonstrated in the exercise 'Comparison of Fourier and convolutional reconstruction algorithms'. For reconstruction of Fresnel holograms, two complementing discrete representations of the optical Fresnel transform exist, the canonical discrete Fresnel transform (DFrT) and the convolutional DFrT. The difference between these transforms is the

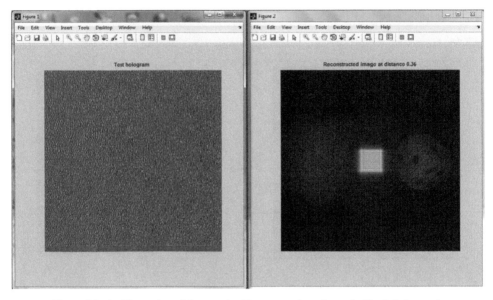

Figure 3.6. An illustration of the exercise 'Reconstruction of a real off-axis hologram'.

sampling strategy. For the canonical DFrT, the image sampling interval Δx in the object plane is equal to $1/\Delta f N$. For the convolutional DFrT, $\Delta x = \Delta f$. The canonical DFrT must be applied for hologram-to-object distances for which the distance parameter of discrete Fresnel transforms $\mu^2 > 1$, the convolutional DFrT when $\mu^2 < 1$. Otherwise, aliasing artifacts appear in reconstruction images. When $\mu^2 = 1$, the two transforms are identical.

Canonical DFrT is implemented by direct use of the fast Fourier transform (FFT); convolutional DFrT is implemented as an FFT-based convolution; hence the names of the algorithms.

The purpose of the exercise 'Comparison of Fourier and convolutional reconstruction algorithms' is to demonstrate hologram sampling aliasing artifacts. The program applies both mentioned transforms for different distances from a real hologram of a test object (two filaments crossed under 90° and part of a ruler, placed at different distances) and displays, frame by frame, corresponding reconstructed images along with a sketch of the test object (to the left of the reconstructed images), on which the reconstruction distance for each particular view is indicated by a segment of horizontal line. Particular examples of displayed results are shown in figure 3.7.

3.4 Image reconstruction from projections

Image reconstruction from projections is an example of the computational imaging that has revolutionized medical diagnostic and non-destructive testing imagings. The exercise 'Image reconstruction from projections' is intended to demonstrate generation of parallel projections of test images and reconstruction of images from their projections using the reconstruction method known as the *'filtered back*

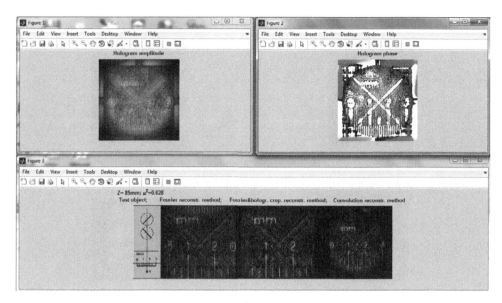

Figure 3.7. An illustration of the exercise 'Comparison of Fourier and convolutional reconstruction algorithms'. A sketch of the test object on the left of the reconstructed images in the bottom image displays, with the help of a moving segment of horizontal line, the distance for which each particular view is obtained.

projection' method. For generating image parallel projections, images are rotated by a sequence of angles from a start angle to an end angle with a step equal to the ratio of the angle range to the number of projections, and then, for each particular rotated image copy, its projection is computed by means of the summation of pixel gray levels along image columns. The angular range and the number of projections are numerical parameters that the user is prompted to define. The whole process is visualized on a computer display.

After completion of the computation of projections of the selected test image, image reconstruction by means of filtered back projection is initiated. Filtered back projection reconstruction consists in (i) computing derivatives of individual projections using 'ramp' filtering (exercises in image differentiation using 'ramp' filtering are described in chapter 4, section 4.6), (ii) projecting the differentiation result at the corresponding angle by means of column-wise replication of its pixels arranged as an image row, (iii) rotation of the obtained 2D array by the given angle and (iv) accumulating the rotated back-projected projection derivatives for the whole angle range. The entire process is visualized on the computer display. For image rotation at both stages of the simulation, the three-step image rotation algorithm described in chapter 4, section 4.4, is used. Upon completion of the reconstruction, an option of displaying the image reconstruction error and its standard deviation normalized to the image dynamic range is offered. Figure 3.8 illustrates images displayed in the exercise.

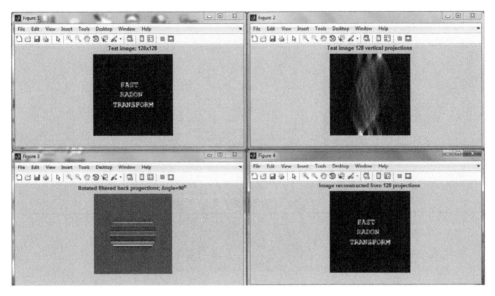

Figure 3.8. An example of images displayed during the exercise 'Image reconstruction from projections'.

3.5 Questions for self-testing

1. How do objects placed at different distances from the hologram affect the reconstructed images of each other?
2. How do the inter-object cross-talk errors of image reconstruction from Fresnel holograms depend on inter-object distances?
3. What physical parameter of the hologram off-axis recording scheme affects the separation of reconstructed images from the zero-order diffraction spot?
4. Why does the image scale change with the distance parameter in hologram reconstruction by the Fourier reconstruction algorithm?
5. How would you describe aliasing artifacts in the reconstruction of Fresnel holograms using the Fourier reconstruction algorithm for $\mu^2 < 1$?
6. How does the error of image reconstruction from projections depend on the number of projections?
7. Were errors of image reconstruction from projections more or less uniform for all tested images? If not, why might this be?

Chapter 4

Image resampling and building continuous image models

4.1 Introduction

Accurate and fast image resampling is a key operation in many digital image processing applications. A few examples are multi-modality data fusion, image mosaicing, image reconstruction from projections, image super-resolution from sequences of image frames, stabilization of videos distorted by turbulence, target location and tracking with sub-pixel accuracy.

Image resampling assumes reconstruction, by means of interpolation of available image samples to obtain samples 'in between' the available ones, of *continuous image models*, i.e. approximations to original non-sampled images, and subsequent sampling of the model. The most feasible interpolation method is digital filtering implemented as a convolution. A number of convolutional interpolation methods are known, beginning from the simplest nearest-neighbor and linear (bilinear, for the 2D case) interpolations to more accurate cubic (bicubic, for the 2D case) and higher-order spline methods. The ultimately accurate method of interpolation of sampled data is the *discrete sinc interpolation* (*sincd interpolation*), which secures 'perfect' interpolation with no interpolation errors except those caused by round-off calculation errors.

This chapter offers exercises in image resampling using perfect image discrete sinc interpolation and its comparison with other known numerical interpolation methods in terms of interpolation accuracy. The exercises are listed in the start menu shown in figure 4.1. The first exercise illustrates the basic principle of signal/image subsampling through successive signal/image fractional shifts. The second exercise demonstrates examples of image geometrical transformation by means of resampling numerical models of initial non-sampled images generated using discrete sinc-interpolated fractional shifts. The third exercise visualizes the work of the fast three-step image rotation algorithm, also implemented through discrete sinc-interpolated fractional shifts. The last two exercises are intended to demonstrate the superiority of the

doi:10.1088/978-0-750-31050-5ch4

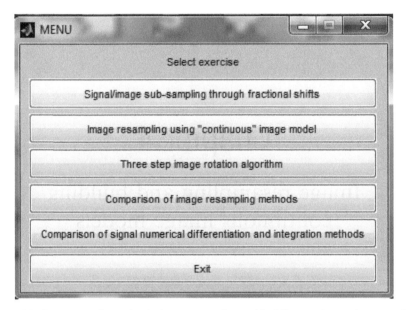

Figure 4.1. Start menu of exercises in image resampling and building continuous image models.

discrete sinc interpolation in comparison with other numerical interpolation methods in terms of interpolation accuracy.

4.2 Signal/image subsampling through fractional shifts

This exercise demonstrates, using as test signals 1D signals and 2D images, the principle of image resampling with discrete sinc interpolation through successive fractional shifts. In the first part of the exercise, 1D interpolation, realizations of pseudo-random signals of 16 samples with a uniform DFT spectrum are used as test signals. Initial signal samples are successively shifted by $1/Lx$ fractions of the sampling interval, where Lx is the signal subsampling rate that the user is prompted to specify. Interpolated values of the shifted signal samples are found by means of discrete sinc interpolation. The core feature of discrete sinc interpolation, its signal spectrum preservation capability, is confirmed by displaying the DFT spectrum of the subsampled signal. The spectrum plot shows that the subsampled signal generated using discrete sinc interpolation is a band-limited signal with band limitation defined by the subsampling rate, and that the uniform spectrum of the initial signal within the limited bandwidth is preserved without any distortions. An example of the display is shown in figure 4.2.

The second part of the exercise, 2D interpolation for image subsampling, is carried out in two steps as a separable interpolation, first over image rows and then over image columns. Both steps are displayed in real time. As test images, a prepared 32 × 32 pixel image 'Eye' and 32 × 32 pixel fragments of images that can be selected by the user are used. The subsampling rate is also a user-defined parameter. Figure 4.3

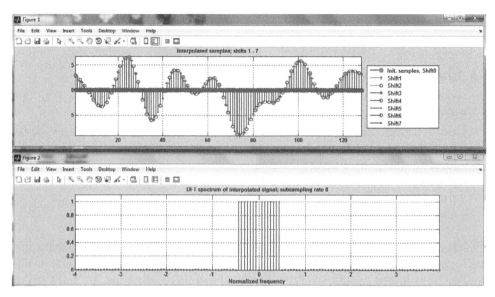

Figure 4.2. 1D signal subsampling through fractional shifts: interpolated signal (top plot) and its band-limited spectrum (bottom plot).

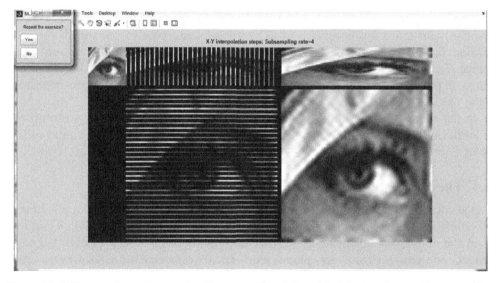

Figure 4.3. 2D image subsampling exercise. Upper part, from left to right: initial test image, this image with a number of zero pixels inserted between initial pixels in the image rows according to the subsampling rate and a result of row-wise interpolation that replaces the zero pixels. Bottom part: row-wise interpolated image with zero rows inserted between image rows according to the subsampling rate (left) and a resulting 2D interpolated image after column-wise interpolation of the row-wise interpolated image (right).

presents an example of displays of the exercise outcomes. It shows the initial test image and results obtained at all steps of its resampling.

4.3 Image resampling using 'continuous' image models

This part of the laboratory offers exercises in using image 'continuous' models generated by means of image subsampling for

- extracting image signal profiles (cross-section) in arbitrary directions specified by the user
- local zooming-in of image fragments
- a general image resampling according to given pixel X/Y displacement pseudo-random maps
- Cartesian-to-polar coordinate conversion.

In each case the user is prompted to select a test image and an image subsampling rate for creating a 'continuous' image model. For extracting the image signal profile, the user is prompted to select, on the displayed test image, first the left and then the right end points of the required profile.

In the 'local zoom exercise', the user is prompted to select, on the displayed test image, a center of the desired image fragment (fragment dimensions are one-eighth of the image dimensions) for zooming and to specify a zoom factor (as a rational number, say, 8/3).

In the exercise 'A general image resampling according to pixel X/Y displacement maps' two options are offered: generating an individual resampled image and generating a sequence of resampled images displayed as a real time video. X/Y pixel displacement maps are generated as 2D arrays, isomorphic to images, of pseudo-random correlated numbers. The map parameters are the number of map 'spots' per image X and Y dimensions and maximal pixel displacement (maximal height of the maps, in pixels). Later, in chapter 6, exercises will be provided that demonstrate how these pseudo-random maps can be generated.

In the exercise 'Cartesian-to-polar coordinate conversion', the user is prompted, in addition to selecting a test image and subsampling rate, to choose a center of the polar coordinate system. Figures 4.4–4.7 illustrate outcomes of these exercises.

4.4 The three-step rotation algorithm

Image rotation is a very frequent operation in many image processing applications. Of course, it can be implemented through resampling of 'continuous' image models as in the above-described exercises. After all, having at hand a 'continuous' image model, one can perform any image geometrical transformation. However, 'continuous' image models generated by means of image subsampling (zooming in) are not ultimately accurate approximations to non-sampled images. Their accuracy depends on the subsampling rate: the higher the subsampling rate, the better the accuracy of the subsequent resampling. Therefore, higher interpolation accuracy requires a higher memory buffer for the storage of subsampled images.

For image rotation, there exists an alternative fast algorithm, the one that enables image rotation to be performed virtually without interpolation errors. This is the

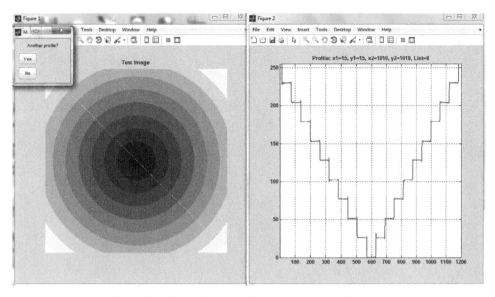

Figure 4.4. Plotting image profiles in user-selected directions.

Figure 4.5. Zooming in of user-selected image fragments.

Figure 4.6. An example of image resampling according to computer-generated pseudo-random pixel displacement *X*/*Y* maps.

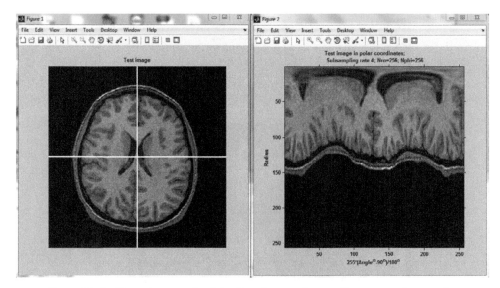

Figure 4.7. An illustrative example of the Cartesian-to-polar coordinate conversion exercise.

so-called *three-step rotation algorithm*. It realizes image rotation through three successive image 'shearings': say, at first in the horizontal direction, then in the vertical direction and finally again in the horizontal direction. In horizontal (vertical) shearing, each image row is shifted by a value which depends on the rotation angle and is also proportional to the row (column) number, counted from the rotation center. For shearing of image rows and columns, the discrete

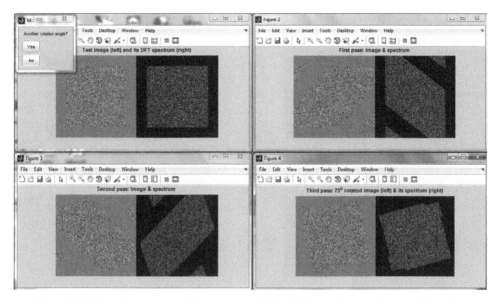

Figure 4.8. Three-step image rotation exercise: rotation aliasing in image and spectral domains.

sinc-interpolation fractional shift algorithm (see the exercise, 'Signal/image sub-sampling through fractional shifts') is perfectly suited.

The present exercise illustrates the work of the algorithm. In image rotation using this algorithm, specific aliasing artifacts may appear when shifted image rows get outside the image frame borders. In order to avoid these artifacts one has to either inscribe the image into an image frame of a larger size in order to create 'safety' borders or split the rotation angle into sufficiently small fractions and carry out rotation successively by these fractional angles. These aliasing artifacts are illustrated using, as test images, two pseudo-random images of different sizes inscribed into an empty image frame of a larger size.

Outcomes of the exercise are exemplified by images in figures 4.8 and 4.9, where all three stages of the algorithm are shown.

4.5 Comparison of image resampling methods

For the comparison of image resampling methods and demonstrating possible interpolation distortions, three exercises are offered:

- Demonstrating point spread functions and impulse responses of different interpolators;
- Multiple rotations of test images;
- Image iterative zooming in/zooming out.

The first exercise in this group, 'Demonstrating point spread functions and frequency responses of different interpolators', is intended solely for the comparison of point spread functions and the discrete frequency responses of regular nearest neighbor (nn), linear (ln) and spline interpolators from MATLAB® signal processing and image processing toolboxes and of the discrete sinc interpolator;

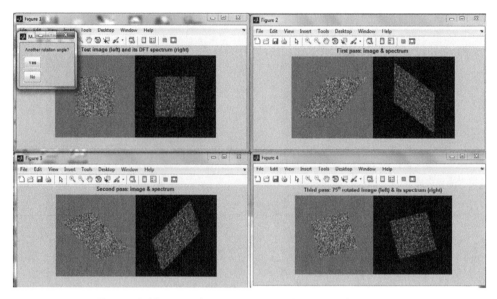

Figure 4.9. Three-step image rotation exercise: no rotation aliasing.

and, in particular, to show that the frequency response of the discrete sinc interpolator is flat within the baseband defined by the sampling rate, whereas the frequency responses of other interpolators are not. Point spread functions and discrete frequency responses of interpolators are useful for analysis and explanation of results of their performance comparison in subsequent exercises. An outcome of this exercise is shown in figure 4.10.

Note that the sample of the frequency response of the discrete sinc interpolator at the signal baseband border is equal to 0.5, and not to 1, which halves the highest frequency component of signals. Such 'spectrum shaping' is a recommended modification of the discrete sinc interpolation made with a purpose of accelerating the discrete sinc function decaying to zero.

The exercise 'Multiple rotations of a test image' is aimed at visual demonstration of losses that may happen in output images due to insufficiently accurate interpolation performed using regular nearest-neighbor, bilinear and bicubic interpolators from MATLAB® toolboxes and of the image preservation capability of the discrete sinc interpolator. For this purpose, a 'text' image and an artificial pseudo-random image with a uniform DFT spectrum within a square of 0.7 times the size of the image frame are used as test images, and test images are subjected to rotations by multiples of 360°, meaning that, ideally, after such rotations, the image must not change. The exercise provides an opportunity to make certain that this is true only for the discrete sinc interpolation. For the 'text' test image, numerical parameters that the user is prompted to select are the number of multiples of 360° rotations and the number of rotation steps per 360°. The program visualizes rotated images as well as rotation errors (the differences between initial and rotated images) and their DFT spectra. The latter are important for understanding the roots of imperfections of compared interpolation algorithms. The work of the program is illustrated in figures 4.11–4.13.

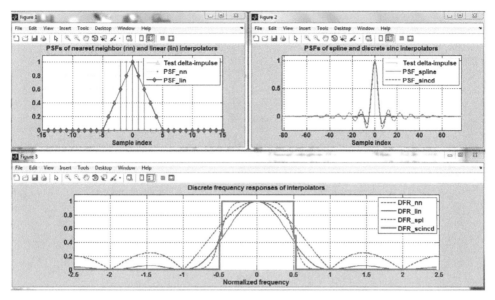

Figure 4.10. Point spread functions and discrete frequency responses (DFRs) of different interpolators. The interval [−0.5 0.5] in plots of discrete frequency responses is the signal baseband defined by its sampling rate.

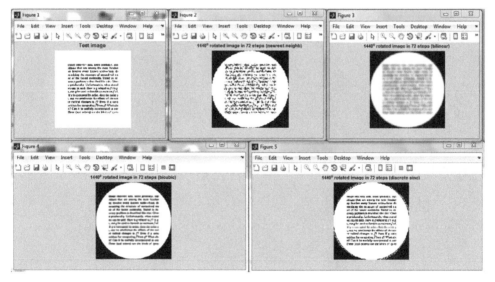

Figure 4.11. Multiple rotations of a test image.

In the exercise with the pseudo-random band-limited image, error power spectra are accumulated for multiple realizations of the test image, which are generated in the course of running the exercise. The number of realizations is a user-defined parameter. An example of the exercise outcome is shown in figure 4.14.

The exercise 'Image iterative zoom-in/zoom-out' is intended for further comparison of the performance of bilinear, bicubic and discrete sinc interpolators. In this exercise, a test image selected by the user is subjected to iterative zooming

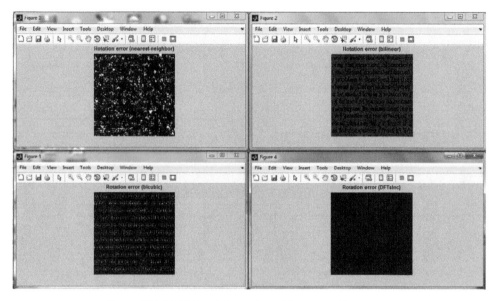

Figure 4.12. Multiple rotations of a test image: rotation errors.

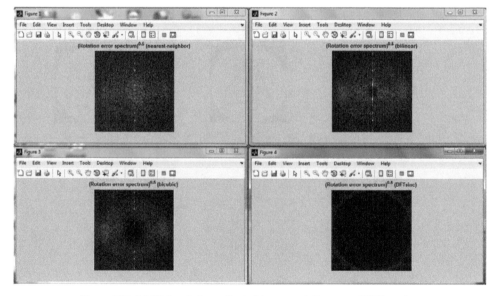

Figure 4.13. Multiple rotations of a test image: rotation error DFT spectra.

in/zooming out with a user-selected zoom-in/zoom-out factor. The number of iterations is also to be specified by the user. As test images, several pre-prepared images, including a pseudo-random uncorrelated image, are offered; in addition, the user can select a test image from his/her own image database. An outcome of the exercise for one of the prepared test images is presented in figure 4.15.

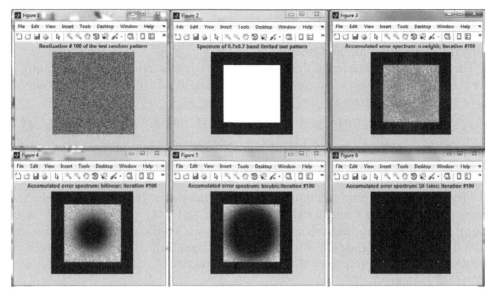

Figure 4.14. Rotation error spectra: pseudo-random test image with uniform DFT spectra.

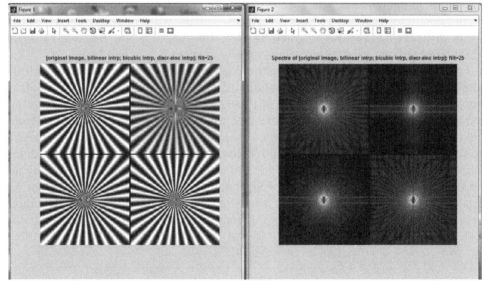

Figure 4.15. Image iterative zoom-in/zoom-out exercise: images (left panel) and their DFT spectra (right panel) displayed as gray scale images centered at the spectrum DC component with the most intensive spectral components shown bright and the least intensive components shown dark.

4.6 Comparison of signal numerical differentiation and integration methods

In the exercise 'Comparison of signal numerical differentiation and integration methods' one can compare the performance of traditional numerical signal differentiation and integration methods and DFT/DCT-based methods that, implicitly, assume signal discrete sinc interpolation and, as such, realize perfect numerical differentiation and integration.

The traditional numerical differentiation methods that are selected for testing in the exercise are the most commonly used ones that, in terms of digital convolution, have point spread functions

$$h_n^{\text{diff}(1)} = [-0.5, 0, 0.5] \quad \text{and} \quad h_n^{\text{diff}(2)} = [-1/12, 8/12, 0, -8/12, 1/12]. \quad (4.1)$$

We refer to these methods as 'd1' and 'd2' methods. Among traditional integration methods, the most commonly used 'trapezoidal' integration method is selected for testing and comparison.

The first exercise in this section is an introductory one. It demonstrates discrete frequency responses of numerical differentiation ('d1', 'd2' and DFT/DCT-based 'ramp filter') and integration (trapezoidal, Simpson, 3/8 Simpson, cubic spline and DFT/DCT-based) methods in order to provide a base for further comparison of the methods and interpretation of the comparison results. A result of this exercise is presented in figure 4.16.

The second exercise is aimed at testing the accuracy of signal differentiation using the d1, d2 differentiation methods and DCT/DFT-based differentiation methods. In order to investigate the dependence of differentiation accuracy on the signal bandwidth, computer-generated pseudo-random signals with uniform DFT spectra within different bandwidths in fractions (1/8, 1/4, 3/8, 1/2, 5/8, 3/4, 7/8, 1) of the signal baseband are used as test signals in the exercise.

Test signals of a user-selected length are generated highly oversampled with the purpose of imitating non-sampled (continuous) signals; the oversampling rate is also a user-selected parameter. Realizations of these oversampled signals are first band limited according to one of the eight above-mentioned fractions of the signal baseband, and their 'ideal' derivatives are computed using the *ramp filter* (the filter with linearly increasing frequency response in the DFT domain) that imitates the analogue differentiation. Then the realizations of the 'ideal' derivative and initial oversampled signals are downsampled with the chosen oversampling rate, and obtained downsampled signals are subjected to differentiation using the above-mentioned traditional methods chosen for testing, as well as using for comparison a DFT-based differentiator.

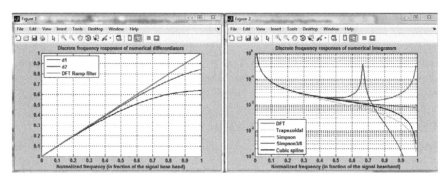

Figure 4.16. Discrete frequency responses of numerical differentiators and integrators.

The ideal sampled derivative is used as a benchmark for computing differentiation errors as sample-by-sample differences between it and the results of the differentiators under comparison. This procedure is repeated several times using different realizations of pseudo-random test signals, and squared differentiation errors are accumulated to obtain good statistical estimates of standard deviations of sample-by-sample differentiation errors. The number of realizations is a user-selected parameter as well.

This procedure can be performed in two versions: without and with an 'apodization mask'. The apodization mask is a window function that is applied as a multiplier to realizations of test signals. It is equal to one everywhere except for a certain number of samples in the vicinity of signal boards, where it gradually decays from one to zero. The purpose of using the apodization mask is to reduce boundary effect errors of the differentiation algorithms.

For each realization, the program displays in one figure plots of realizations of test signals, their ideal derivatives and those obtained by the DFT method, and in another figure plots of estimates of standard deviations of sample-by-sample differentiation errors for all tested methods, the estimates being accumulated over the iteration steps. After completion of the evaluation of differentiation errors for all realizations of signals of all bandwidths, the program displays final estimates of standard deviations of sample-wise errors as well as plots of the standard deviation of differentiation errors evaluated over three-quarters of the length of the signals with an exclusion of one-eighth of the signal samples closest to the left and right signal borders (for excluding boundary effect errors), as shown in figure 4.17. The graphs are plotted versus test signal bandwidths.

The third exercise in this section performs simultaneous testing of both differentiation and integration methods through repetitive test signal successive

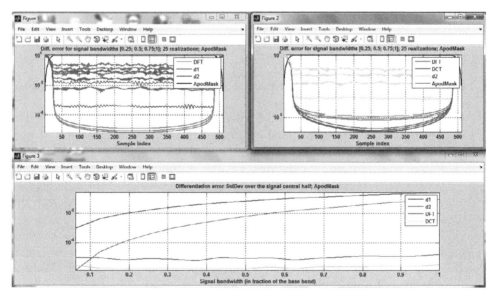

Figure 4.17. The final output display of the differentiator comparison exercise.

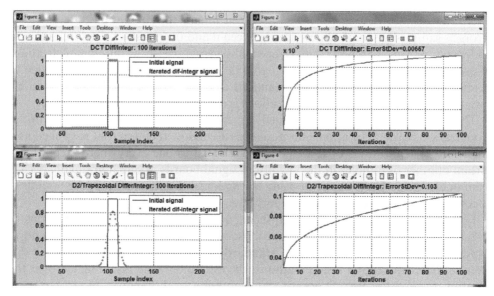

Figure 4.18. Test signal iterative differentiation/integration.

differentiation and integration performed in tandem. Ideally, signals should not be changed by such processing. The exercise is intended to show that this is the case only when signal derivatives and integrals are computed by DFT/DCT-based algorithms, whereas conventional numerical differentiation and integration algorithms after multiple applications result in considerable signal blur. The number of differentiation/integration steps is a user-defined parameter. All steps are visualized by plots of initial and processed test signals and of signal reproduction root mean square error as a function of the number of iterations. An exemplar of an outcome of the exercise is shown in figure 4.18.

4.7 Questions for self-testing

1. Why is image interpolation needed for extracting image signal arbitrary profiles?
2. In what application might it be useful and computationally efficient to generate subsampled (zoomed-in) images to use as digital models of non-sampled images?
3. Have you noticed oscillations in the vicinity of object edges that occasionally appear in resampled images, such as those seen in figures 4.3 and 4.4? How would you explain these artifacts? At what price can one prevent the appearance of these artifacts?
4. In what applications might Cartesian-to-polar image coordinate conversion be useful or required?
5. Explain the meaning of rotation error spectra in the exercise 'Multiple rotations of a test image'.
6. Explain aliasing artifacts in spectra of rotated images.

7. What is your interpretation of test image spectra in the exercise 'Image iterative zoom-in/zoom-out'?
8. What are signal degradations in numerical differentiation and integration and why are these degradations absent for DFT/DCT-based algorithms?
9. What conclusions regarding practical applications of different numerical differentiators and integrators can be made from comparison of their frequency responses?
10. When for signal integration Simpson and 3/8 Simpson integration methods are used, which artifacts can one expect based on the frequency response of the methods?
11. Is it possible to further improve the image interpolation accuracy beyond that achieved by the discrete sinc interpolation?

Chapter 5

Image and noise statistical characterization and diagnostics

5.1 Introduction

The set of exercises 'Image and noise statistical characterization and diagnostics' is aimed at assisting the study of concepts and methods of statistical characterization of images and noise, which is usually present in image signals and distorts them. Statistical characterization means measuring and using parameters and characteristics that do not specify concrete pixels or images, but rather refer to properties common to groups of pixels or images, which enables solution of processing optimization problems for these groups. A large variety of statistical parameters and characteristics exists. For exercises we selected in this chapter the most frequently used ones listed in the main menu presented in figure 5.1.

5.2 Image histograms

One of the primary statistical characteristics of images is the histogram of pixel gray levels. Image histograms show how frequently different gray levels occur in a particular image. One should distinguish global histograms measured over the entire image frame and 'local' histograms that are measured over a certain, most commonly spatial, neighborhood of each pixel. This is what the subject of this section is. Later in section 5.4 some other types of neighborhood will be discussed and experimented with. In chapter 8 ('Methods of image perfection') and chapter 9 ('Methods of image enhancement'), we will see that local image histograms computed for other types of pixel neighborhood are also important for implementing image nonlinear filters.

The exercise 'Image histograms' provided in this section enables comparison of global (frame-wise) histograms for different images as well as observation of the variability of the image local histogram. The latter is achieved by means of visualizing mean square deviations and maximal deviations of image local histograms from the local histogram of the user-selected image fragment. Horizontal and vertical

Figure 5.1. Image and noise statistical characterization and diagnostics: main menu.

dimensions of the rectangular window for computing local histograms are user-selected parameters. These pixel-wise deviations are displayed as images homomorphic with the selected test image along with their numerical measures: maximal mean square and maximum of maximal deviations over the entire image. One can use these numerical measures for evaluation of the variability of local histograms in different test images. Also plotted are the image global histogram and the histogram of the selected reference image fragment. To conduct the exercise, three options are offered for selecting a test image: two pre-prepared images, a face image and a texture image, and any other image from the user's image data set. Figure 5.2 illustrates outcomes of this exercise.

5.3 Image local moments and order statistics

Image local histograms are arrays of 256 numbers for every pixel, i.e. they are vectorial parameters. Much more compact statistical descriptors are scalar histogram parameters and their moments, such as mean value and standard deviation. Another alternative to histograms is the so-called *order statistics*, pixel array gray levels sorted in an ascending order into a sequence called a *variational row*.

The variational row spans from the minimal gray level in the array, and this is the first term of the row, to the gray level maximum, the last term of the row. The size of the row is equal to the number of pixels in the array. The term in the middle of the variational row is the so-called median: it is the gray level for which the numbers of

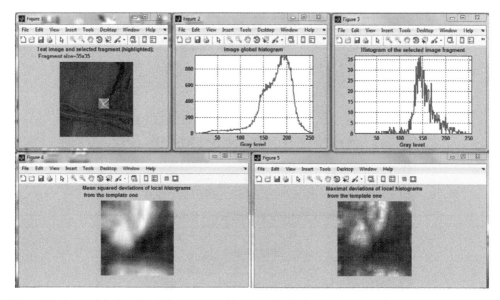

Figure 5.2. Image global and local histograms and 'maps' of deviations of image local histograms over 35 × 35 pixel windows from the local histogram of the highlighted fragment.

pixels of lower and of higher gray values are equal. The median is known as an estimate of mean value over the array that is robust to outliers.

The exercise 'Image local moments and order statistics' is intended for visualizing these parameters. Displayed are test images selected by the user and their local means, local medians, local standard deviations, local maxima, local minima and local maxima minus minima (*local range*) in a running window. Horizontal and vertical dimensions of the window are to be set by the user. An illustrative example of the visualized mentioned local statistical parameters is presented in figure 5.3.

5.4 Pixel attributes and neighborhoods

All pixels in image arrays have certain attributes that are used in the design of image processing filters. The obvious primary pixel attributes are pixel coordinates in image arrays and pixel gray levels. There are also many other attributes, less obvious but nevertheless proved to be useful. The exercise 'Pixel attributes and neighborhoods' is intended for studying pixel attributes associated with image histograms and for studying pixel neighborhoods as groups of pixels unified in terms of certain attributes.

Attributes associated with image histograms are *pixel cardinality* and *pixel rank*. Pixel cardinality is the number of pixels in the pixel array that have the same gray level as the given pixel. Pixel rank is an index of the pixel in the variational row, i.e. the number of pixels in the array that have gray levels lower than the gray level of the given pixel. Pixel cardinalities and ranks can be computed globally over the entire image frame or locally in a moving window.

In the exercise, these attributes are given in the entrance menu under the label 'Pixel statistical attributes'. After loading a test image, global cardinalities and ranks

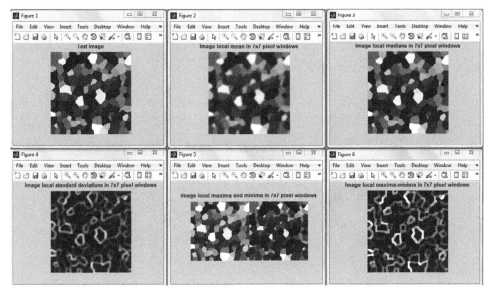

Figure 5.3. Image local mean, medians, standard deviations, maxima, minima and range.

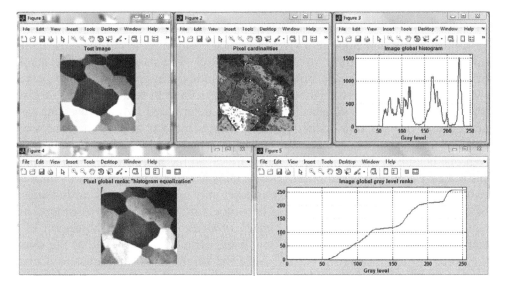

Figure 5.4. Pixel global cardinalities and ranks.

are displayed in the form of images homomorphic to the test image. After this the user is prompted to choose an option of displaying local pixel attributes in a running window and set the dimensions of the window. Figures 5.4 and 5.5 present examples of outcomes of the exercise.

Note that the replacement of pixels with their rank is a procedure called *histogram equalization*. Later in chapter 9 the use of this procedure and its modifications for image enhancement will be demonstrated.

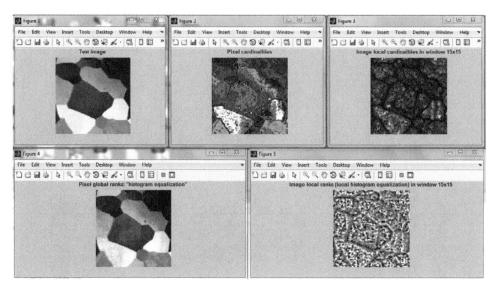

Figure 5.5. Pixel global and local cardinalities.

Pixel neighborhood is a very important notion in the design of image processing algorithms. A neighborhood of a given pixel is a group of pixels of the same image unified in terms of a certain attribute of the pixel. The most relevant are neighborhoods formed from pixels from a certain window centered at the given pixel. A variety of types of pixel neighborhood can be defined in terms of different pixel attributes. The relevance of specific attributes is determined by the processing task and end user *a priori* knowledge regarding imaged objects and by the processing goal. For instance, in many cases one can believe that pixels spatially closest to the given one belong to the same object. They are called the pixel *spatial neighborhood.* This is a very common assumption. More sophisticated are neighborhoods built on the basis of other pixel attributes such as pixel gray levels, rank and cardinalities.

For gray levels as pixel attributes, two types of so-called *V-neighborhood* are defined: *EV-neighborhoods* and *KNV-neighborhoods.* The EV-neighborhood of a pixel with a gray level V unifies window pixels with gray levels within the range $[V - \varepsilon V_-, V + \varepsilon V_+]$, where $\{\varepsilon V_-, \varepsilon V_+\}$ are the neighborhood parameters. Correspondingly, the KNV-neighborhood of a pixel unifies K window pixels with gray levels closest to the gray value V of that pixel. K is the neighborhood parameter.

Similarly, for pixel ranks as pixel attributes, *R-neighborhoods* can be defined: the *ER-neighborhood* of a pixel with rank R as a set of window pixels with ranks in the range $[R - \varepsilon R_-, R + \varepsilon R_+]$ with $\{\varepsilon R_-, \varepsilon R_+\}$ as neighborhood parameters and the *KNR-neighborhood* as a set of K window pixels with ranks closest to R, i.e. with ranks in the range $[R - (K - 1)/2, R + (K - 1)/2]$. Obviously, the KNR-neighborhood is a special case of the ER-neighborhood.

For cardinalities as pixel attributes, the *cluster neighborhood* (Cl-neighborhood) of a pixel is defined as a subset of window pixels with cardinalities that belong to the same cluster of the window histogram as the given pixel. By clusters, consolidated peaks, or hills, of histograms are meant.

In the exercise 'Pixel neighborhoods', the user is first prompted to select one of two prepared test images or an arbitrary image from the user image database and set the horizontal and vertical dimensions of an image fragment, which will be used for visualizing neighborhoods of the fragment central pixel. Then the user is prompted to select, using a cross-cursor, the center of an image fragment to work with. The selected fragment and its gray level histogram are displayed together with a list of types of neighborhood. Upon selecting the neighborhood type, the neighborhood of the fragment central pixel is displayed in the bottom right panel with pixels not belonging to the neighborhood shown black. In addition, borders of the neighborhood are indicated on plots of the fragment histogram (for V- and Cl-neighborhoods) or fragment variational row (for R-neighborhoods), as illustrated in figures 5.6–5.9.

In the case of the cluster neighborhood, the user is also prompted to select, using a cursor on the plot of the fragment histogram, left and right borders of the histogram cluster to which the fragment central pixel is believed to belong.

5.5 Image autocorrelation functions and power spectra

Image autocorrelation functions and power spectra complement each other as image statistical characteristics that carry information on the spatial interdependence of pixel gray levels. The most common feature of images is that image correlation functions decay relatively slowly with the distance over which pixel correlations are measured, and image power spectra in some bases, such as those of DFT, DCT and

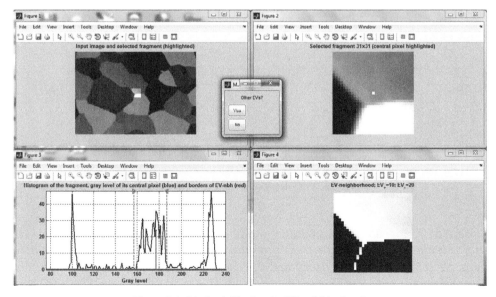

Figure 5.6. Pixel neighborhoods: EV-neighborhood.

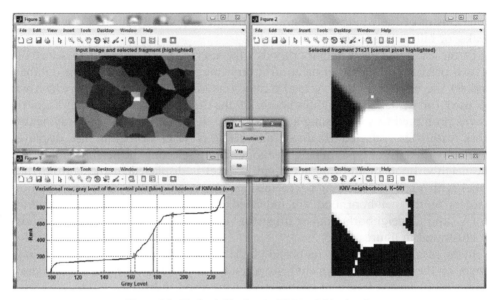

Figure 5.7. Pixel neighborhoods: KNV-neighborhood.

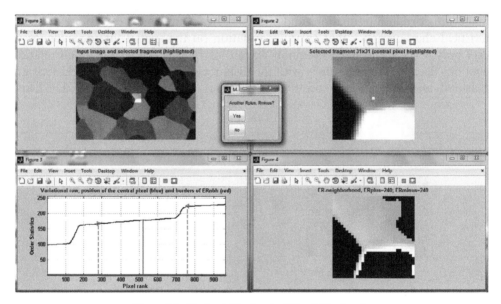

Figure 5.8. Pixel neighborhoods: ER-neighborhood.

Walsh transforms, decay considerably rapidly with spectral coefficient indices. The latter is a manifestation of the transform energy compaction capabilities studied in chapter 2. The speed of the decay and the shapes of autocorrelation functions and power spectra are in a certain way associated with a kind of 'average' size and shape of objects in images.

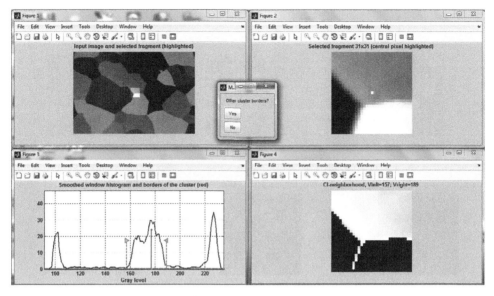

Figure 5.9. Pixel neighborhoods: Cl-neighborhood.

The set of exercises 'Image autocorrelation functions and power spectra' is intended for studying these features and associations. In the exercise 'Image auto-correlation functions', the user can select as test images either three prepared images (an artificial computer-generated piece-wise constant image, a microscopic image of blood cells and an air photograph) or one of the images from his/her image database. The program displays, in the form of images, 2D arrays of image autocorrelation functions and, as an option, the same arrays uniformly quantized in ten levels that represent ten levels of autocorrelation function magnitude. In the latter case quantized autocorrelation functions are displayed, to better visualize autocorrelation function level lines, color coded using a MATLAB® color map 'jet', as shown in figure 5.10 of test images and their correlation functions.

In the exercise 'Image power spectra', DCT image global and local spectra are visualized. As test images, three images ('geometrical figures', 'angular step wedge' and 'camera man') are offered. The user can also select any other test image from his/her image database. Global spectra are visualized color coded using a color map 'jet' in order to make visible low-intensity high-frequency image spectral components (figure 5.11). Local spectra are shown for image blocks (figure 5.12). Block vertical and horizontal dimensions are to be set by the user.

5.6 Image noise

Image noise is a very important factor that may substantially hamper image usage. One of the primary image processing tasks is image cleaning from noise. In order to enable image denoising, one should know numerical parameters that can sufficiently well characterize the noise component of the image signal and its influence on image 'readability'. Though contamination of image signals by noise

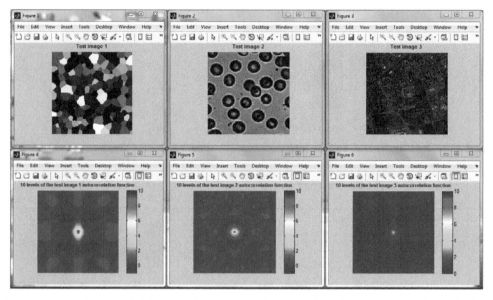

Figure 5.10. Test images and their correlation functions (shown as color-coded images with color coding bar to the side).

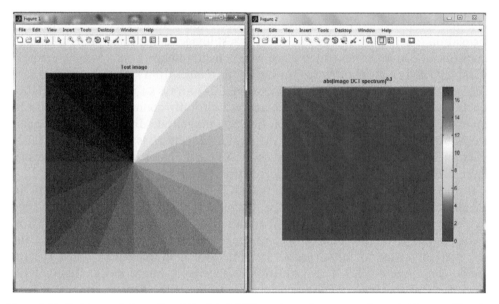

Figure 5.11. Test image (left panel) and its global DCT spectrum shown as a color-coded image with color coding bar to the side (right panel).

may be caused by different factors, such as quantum fluctuations of radiation used for imaging, thermal fluctuations of electrical current in image sensors, failures in communication systems used for transmitting image signals, mechanical instabilities in image scanners, variations of sensitivity of individual photo sensitive cells in

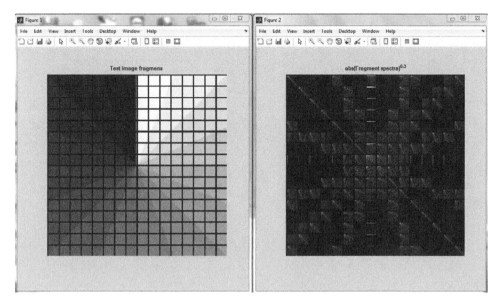

Figure 5.12. Spectra (right panel) of corresponding fragments of a test image (left panel).

photographic cameras etc, three basic mathematical noise models are in most cases sufficient for developing noise cleaning methods: *additive signal independent noise*, *impulsive signal independent noise* and *signal dependent noise*.

The set of exercises 'Image noise' is intended for the demonstration of these typical noise models, for experimentations with the 'visibility' of different types of noise and for practicing with the automated evaluation of noise numerical parameters on noised images. Implemented are (i) three types of additive noise—wide-band (uncorrelated) signal independent *normal white noise* and two types of narrow-band noise, *banding noise* and *moiré noise*, (ii) impulsive noise and (iii) *speckle noise*. The latter is an example of signal dependent noise.

In the first exercise of this group, 'Additive noise', which includes demonstrations of wide-band and narrow-band noise, three test images are offered: 'circular step wedge', 'air photograph' and 'space photograph'. The user can also use any other image from his/her image database. The user has also to set the noise standard deviation in units of image dynamic range 0–255. Figure 5.13 illustrates the case of broadband noise.

As for narrow-band additive noise, two types of noise are simulated: banding noise and moiré noise. The banding noise is implemented in its simplest form: image rows are distorted by adding to all the pixels of each row a zero-mean random value uniformly distributed in the range specified by the user (in gray levels). The program visualizes different realizations of the banding noise on the selected test image. An example is shown in figure 5.14.

Moiré noise is a type of additive noise with relatively small numbers of isolated DFT or DCT spectral components. In the exercise, it is simulated by means of generating, in random positions in the DCT domain, a number specified by the user

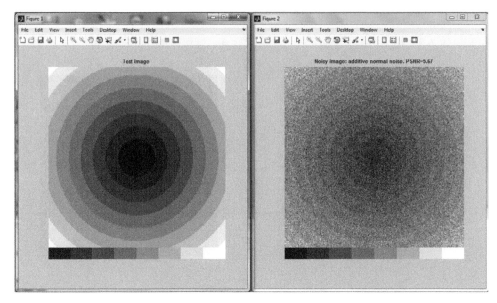

Figure 5.13. Image noise exercise: test image (left panel) and image with added broadband normal noise with peak signal-to-noise ratio (PSNR) 5.67 (right panel).

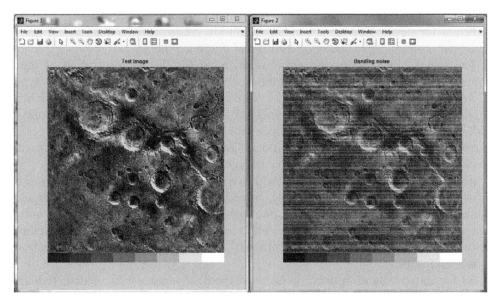

Figure 5.14. Image noise exercise: test image (left panel) and image with narrow-band noise, the banding noise (right panel).

of moiré noise spectral components with random intensities, with maximal intensity also specified by the user. Similarly to the case of banding noise, the program allows visualization of different realizations of moiré noise on test images selected by the user. An example is presented in figure 5.15.

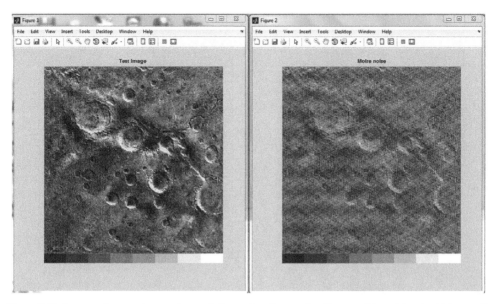

Figure 5.15. Image noise exercise: test image (left panel) and example of image with moiré noise (right panel).

Impulsive noise causes the replacement of gray levels of individual pixels, randomly selected with some probability called the probability of error, by a random value taken from the image dynamic range 0–255. In the exercise 'Impulsive noise' the user, besides selecting a test image, has to specify the probability of error. After this the program displays the image distorted by the impulsive noise and this can be repeated with different realizations of noise on the same test image. An example of the display is shown in figure 5.16.

Signal dependent image noise is exemplified in this exercise by speckle noise. Speckle noise is an image distortion characteristic of imaging using coherent radiation, such as holographic, synthetic aperture radar and ultrasound imaging. In a distinction from noise in conventional incoherent imaging systems, for instance photography, speckle noise originates not from random quantum fluctuations of radiation or from thermal fluctuations of sensor array current, but rather from signal distortions in radiation recording devices such as limitation of their resolving power or signal quantization or limitation of the recoded signal dynamic range. The chaotic character of speckle noise is associated with the chaotic character of the object reflectance or transmittance phase component due to roughness of the surface or other factors that affect phase variations of coherent radiation reflected or transmitted by objects.

The program that imitates speckle noise simulates recording Fourier holograms with the following types of distortion in signal recording:

- limitation of the hologram size, which is equivalent to limitation of the holographic imaging resolving power;
- limitation of the dynamic range of the hologram orthogonal (sinusoidal and cosinusoidal) components;
- quantization of the hologram orthogonal components.

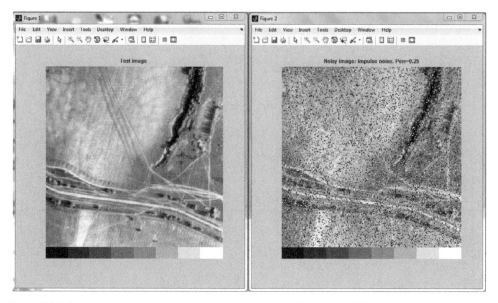

Figure 5.16. Image noise exercise: test image (left panel) and example of image with impulsive noise (right panel).

As a test signal, a circular step wedge image is offered; the user has also an option of selecting another test image from his/her image database. Test images specify imaged object intensity. The image intensity component is supplemented, by the simulation program, with a pseudo-random uncorrelated phase component uniformly distributed in $(-\pi, \pi)$ that imitates the object surface roughness. Upon selection of a test image, the user is prompted to select the type of hologram distortion.

For limitation of the hologram size, the user has to specify a fraction (between 0 and 1) of the whole hologram retained for image reconstruction. The simulation program then displays the trimmed hologram, the reconstructed image and plots of middle rows of the initial and reconstructed image (figure 5.17).

For the dynamic range limitation, the user is prompted to specify the hologram dynamic range in terms of the ratio (from two to five) of the hologram recording device dynamic range to the standard deviation σ of the hologram orthogonal components. For the hologram quantization, the user has to set the number of uniform quantization levels in the dynamic range of $[-4\sigma, 4\sigma]$. Figures 5.18 and 5.19 show examples of the corresponding displays.

5.7 Empirical diagnostics of image noise

For the design of image denoising algorithms, numerical data on statistical parameters of noise in image signals are needed. Sometimes these data are available in certificates of imaging systems provided by system producers. When they are not, as it frequently happens in applications, one needs to extract the necessary data from available images. This is quite a tricky problem, a kind of vicious circle: in order to

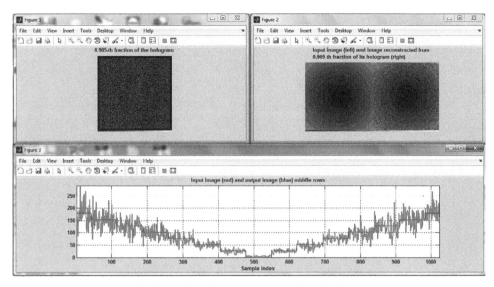

Figure 5.17. Speckle noise exercise: limitation of hologram size.

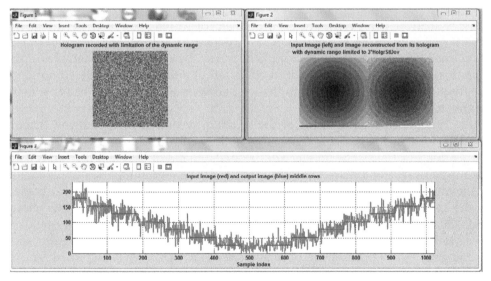

Figure 5.18. Speckle noise exercise: limitation of hologram dynamic range.

measure the statistical parameters of noise present in images one needs to separate noise from signals, but knowledge of noise statistical parameters is required for this separation.

The way out of this vicious circle is not to separate noise from signals but rather to separate their statistical characteristics. In a number of cases the latter is possible with the help of quite simple means. The core idea is to measure

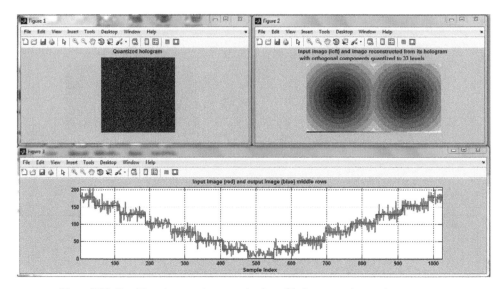

Figure 5.19. Speckle noise exercise: quantization of hologram orthogonal components.

those statistical characteristics of the image distorted by noise, in which the presence of noise exhibits itself as an easily detected anomaly. The set of exercises 'Empirical diagnostics of image noise' illustrates this approach on examples of the empirical evaluation of the standard deviation of additive uncorrelated noise, of the frequencies and intensity of moiré noise components and of the banding noise parameters in images.

For automated measurement of the standard deviation of broadband (uncorrelated) noise in images it is frequently sufficient to measure noisy image autocorrelation functions. The presence in the image signal of such noise exhibits itself in the appearance of a sharp anomalous peak in the image autocorrelation function at the origin of its coordinate, which corresponds to no shift between image copies. In the exercise, the user can select either of two prepared test images ('air photo' and 'face') or any other image from the image database, and set the standard deviation of additive uncorrelated normal noise. The simulation program adds to the image a realization of normal noise with the given standard deviation and displays the noisy image and graphs of a central cross-section of the noisy image autocorrelation function and of the estimated noise correlation function. The latter is a delta function weighted by the estimate of the noise standard deviation. The separation of noise and the image autocorrelation function is made by means of parabolic extrapolation of samples with indices 2 and 3 of the noisy image autocorrelation function, which correspond to shifts by 2 and 3 sampling intervals, to its first sample, which corresponds to no shift. The difference between the actual squared value of the autocorrelation function first sample and its extrapolated value is taken as an estimate of the additive noise variance. Figure 5.20 illustrates an outcome of the exercise.

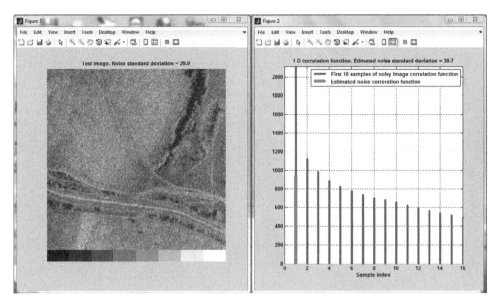

Figure 5.20. Empirical diagnostics of image noise exercise: diagnostics of additive normal noise.

The characteristic indication of the presence in images of moiré noise is the presence of more or less isolated anomalously large sharp peaks in the image power spectra. These peaks can be quite easily detected in the difference between the actual spectrum and its smoothed copy, in which the noise peaks are suppressed. This principle is implemented and illustrated in the exercise. The program first displays two prepared test images with real (not simulated) moiré noise and prompts the user to select one of these images or to download another image from the user's image database. Once a test image is selected, it is displayed for viewing along with, in another figure window, the DFT row-wise power spectrum of the selected test image averaged over all image rows. Then the user is prompted to set a threshold for detecting anomalous peaks in the displayed spectrum, assuming that these peaks might be spectral components of moiré noise. The recommended range of the threshold is [0.01–0.1]. It is used by the program for detecting violations of 'monotonicity' of the spectrum decay with frequency index. The detection is carried out by means of comparing differences between the intensities of spectral components with adjacent indices with this threshold in the course of their analysis from low-frequency to high-frequency components. At frequencies where violations of monotonicity are detected, the spectrum intensity is replaced by its value at the previous frequency index. In this way, a smoothed spectrum is formed. It is plotted in the upper subplot of the figure along with a plot of the initial spectrum. The difference between the initial and smoothed spectra represents estimates of the spectrum of the supposed moiré noise. This is plotted for visual evaluation in the bottom subplot of the figure (figure 5.21). The user is then prompted either to select another detection threshold or to finish the exercise.

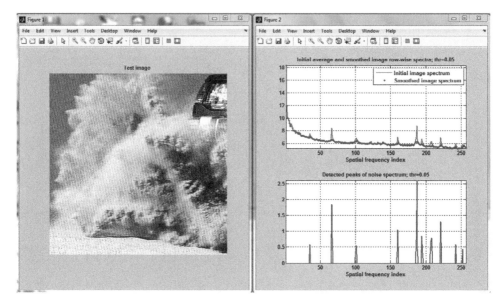

Figure 5.21. Empirical diagnostics of image noise exercise: diagnostics of moiré noise.

In the exercises of chapter 8 one will see how these estimates can be used for filtering out moiré noise.

As has been mentioned, banding noise is caused by adding to all pixels of each individual image rows the same random values. Therefore the diagnostics of banding noise assumes the determination of these random additions to image rows. This can be done with the assumption that mean values of individual image rows do not normally, in the absence of banding noise, change considerably from row to row; i.e. image row mean values regarded as a function of row indices are sufficiently smooth functions. This implies that smoothing the sequence of means of image rows contaminated with banding noise may provide a reasonably good estimate of the noiseless sequence and the difference between the two will be a good estimate of values that distort image rows. This idea is implemented in the program that supports the exercise. For smoothing, local mean filtering is employed. The filter works in a window sliding over the sequence under filtering, and in each window position replaces the actual value of the window central sample by the mean value of the samples within the window. Window size is a filter parameter that is to be set by the user.

For experimentation, two options are offered: either to download an arbitrary test image from the image database and work with simulated banding noise or to open a prepared test image distorted by real banding noise, a sample image produced by an atomic force microscope. If the simulated banding noise option is selected, the selected test image is displayed in one figure and the user is prompted to set the dynamic range of the banding noise (as a fraction of the image dynamic range 0–255). Then the selected image with simulated banding noise is displayed and its row-wise means are plotted in another figure window versus the row index. If the second option of an

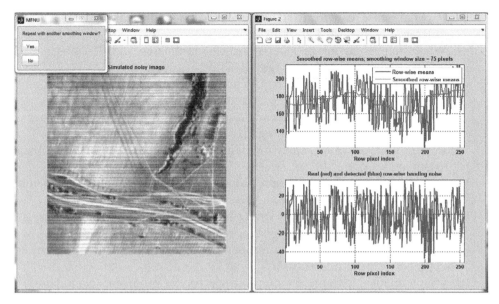

Figure 5.22. Empirical diagnostics of image noise exercise: diagnostics of banding noise.

image with real banding noise is selected, such a display appears immediately. In order to proceed to the noise diagnostics, the user is then prompted to set a window size of the median filter for smoothing the image row-wise means. Once this is done, the smoothed row-wise means are plotted on the same upper subplot as is the initial sequence of row-wise means, and the difference between the two, which represents an estimate of the banding noise realization, is plotted in the lower subplot. In the case of simulated banding noise, actual values of the simulated noise are plotted as well for the comparison and evaluation of the efficiency of the estimate. In chapter 8 there will be another opportunity to test the efficiency of the described method for filtering out banding noise. Figure 5.22 illustrates an outcome of the exercise.

5.8 Questions for self-testing

1. Are histograms of different images similar to each other?
2. Are there images homogeneous in terms of local histograms? If so, which types of image are?
3. Can one detect objects in images by means of comparing their histograms with image local histograms within fragments of the corresponding size?
4. Sometimes one can detect clusters (consolidated peaks, or 'hills') in image histograms. How can they be interpreted?
5. How would you describe differences between local means and local medians?
6. What image local statistical characteristics can be used for edge detection?
7. What information about images is contained in the differences between image local maxima and minima?

8. In what sense can local standard deviation and local maxima–minima difference be regarded as akin?

9. What changes in image local statistical parameters did you observe for different window sizes in images of different types?

10. How well, in your opinion, do different types of pixel neighborhood unify pixels that belong to the same object?

11. In addition to pixel gray levels and ranks, would you suggest any other pixel attributes as a basis for forming pixel neighborhoods?

12. In your opinion, may displaying image local pixel attributes help in image visual analysis?

13. Have you appreciated any connections between shapes of image correlation functions and shapes of objects present in images?

14. Have you appreciated the variability of image local spectra? Is this variability characteristic for all types of image?

15. Where is the energy compaction capability of transforms more pronounced, in global or in local spectra?

16. Can numerical parameters of local spectra be promising candidates for defining local spectrum-based pixel attributes?

17. In your opinion, what kind of noise, additive normal broadband, moiré noise, banding noise or impulsive noise, is most destructive for image readability, assuming that all of them have the same standard deviation?

18. What kind of noise, additive, multiplicative or impulsive, is speckle noise caused by the limitation of the imaging system resolving power? What will be the answer to this question for speckle noise caused by other distortions of hologram recording devices?

19. In your opinion, how does the accuracy of the empirical estimation of the intensity of additive broadband noise depend on the image content?

20. Which is easier to detect, low-frequency or high-frequency moiré noise components?

Chapter 6

Statistical image models and pattern formation

6.1 Introduction

Statistical image models are mathematical models for generating pseudo-random images with certain prescribed statistical properties. They are used in simulations of imaging systems and testing image processing algorithms as well as for the synthesis of artificial images that imitate natural ones. The exercises in this chapter demonstrate an algorithmic approach to building statistical image models, according to which the models are built through certain (specific for each model) combinations of a set of certain standard elementary operations applied in a certain order to a starting, or seed, image. Implemented here are the following models listed in the entrance menu of the exercise (figure 6.1).

- Point-wise nonlinearity (PWN) model: seed images are subjected, pixel by pixel, to a point-wise nonlinear transformation specified by its amplitude transfer function.
- Linear filter (LF) model: seed images are subjected to a linear filtering with a certain prescribed point spread function or frequency response.
- Point-wise nonlinearity and linear filter (PWN&LF) model: seed images are first subjected to a point-wise nonlinear transformation and then to a linear filtering.
- Linear filter and point-wise nonlinearity (LF&PWN) model: seed images are first subjected to a linear filtering and then to a point-wise nonlinear transformation.
- Evolutionary models, i.e. models with a feedback: seed images used as inputs to an iterative filtering specific for the model are, at each iteration step, images obtained at the previous iteration step.

All exercises display resulting synthetic images for visual evaluation.

6.2 PWN models

Point-wise nonlinearity (PWN) models are the simplest ones in the family of image statistical models and pattern generators. Using point-wise transformation, one can

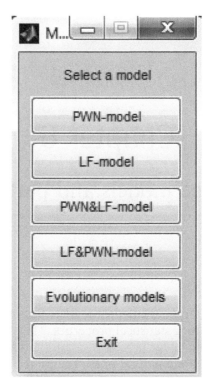

Figure 6.1. Statistical image models and pattern formation: the entrance menu.

control the probability histograms of output images, and this is the only image statistical parameter that can be controlled. The following three versions of PWN models are implemented.

- Generation of binary pseudo-random images with probabilities of 'one' proportional, for each pixel, to the gray level normalized to unity of the corresponding, i.e. having the same coordinate, pixel of a reference image. The resulting images are, naturally, spatially inhomogeneous according to the spatial inhomogeneity of the reference images. As seed images, arrays of pseudo-random numbers with uniform distribution obtained using the standard MATLAB® generator of 'random' numbers are used. The nonlinearity used is a threshold nonlinearity, the threshold being equal, for each particular pixel, to the normalized gray levels of the corresponding pixel of the reference image. Reference images are to be selected by the user from the user's image database. An example of patterns generated by the model is shown in figure 6.2.

- Generation of zero-mean pseudo-random images with normal distribution and standard deviation proportional, for each pixel, to the normalized gray level of the corresponding pixel of a reference image. Resulting pseudo-random images are simulated realizations of signal dependent multiplicative noise. As seed images, pseudo-random numbers with normal distribution taken from the standard MATLAB® pseudo-random number generator are used. The amplitude transfer function of the 'nonlinearity' is a linear transfer

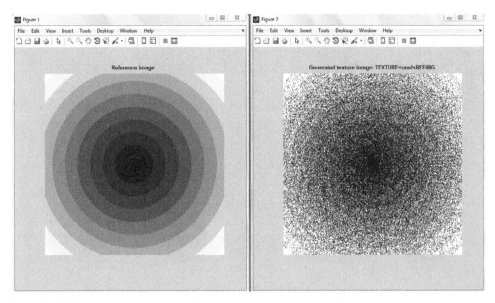

Figure 6.2. PWN model: an example of a binary pseudo-random image with spatial variant densities of 'one'.

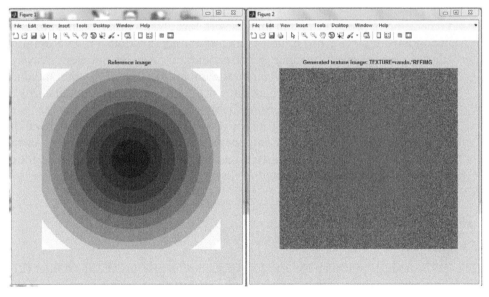

Figure 6.3. PWN model: a reference image (left panel) and an example of a pseudo-random image with pixel standard deviations proportional to the gray levels of corresponding pixels of the reference image (right panel).

function, which spans the image dynamic range ([0–255]) with a slope proportional, for each particular pixel of the output image, to the gray level of the corresponding pixel of the reference image. As in the previous exercise, reference images are to be selected by the user. Figure 6.3 presents an example of an image generated in this way and its corresponding reference image.

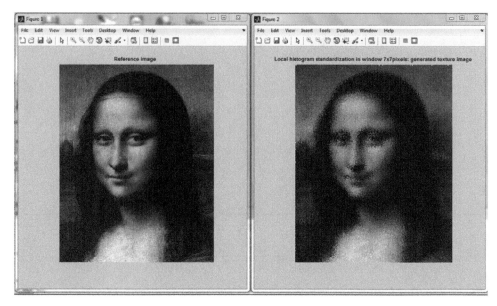

Figure 6.4. PWN model: an example of a pseudo-random image with local histograms over a certain window identical to local histograms of the reference images in corresponding window positions.

- Generation of pseudo-random images with local histograms identical to local histograms of a reference image in corresponding positions of windows used for computing reference image local histograms. As seed images, arrays of uniformly distributed pseudo-random numbers generated by the standard MATLAB® random number generator are used. The model nonlinearity is the one that converts the uniform distribution of pseudo-random numbers to the gray level distribution histogram of the corresponding fragment of the reference image. The reference images as well as X and Y dimensions of the window for computing local histograms are to be set by the user. A result of the use of the model is presented in figure 6.4.

6.3 LF models

6.3.1 Introduction

While PWN models control image gray level distribution histograms, linear filter (LF) models generate images with pre-defined power spectra (or, alternatively, auto-correlation functions). It is noteworthy that, by virtue of the central limit theorem of the probability theory, gray level distributions of images generated by LF models tend to a normal (Gaussian) distribution.

Exercises in this section demonstrate synthesized images for several types of image spectrum and a possibility of generating images that imitate certain types of natural texture. The models are implemented directly in spectral DFT or DCT domains through multiplying seed arrays of pseudo-random uncorrelated zero-mean numbers with a uniform distribution in the range [−0.5, 0.5] from the standard

MATLAB® random number generator by spectral masks of certain selected forms or controlled by a reference image. In this way, the power spectrum of the generated images is specified by the spectral masks, while their chaotic character is specified by the pseudo-random numbers.

6.3.2 Textures with circular 'ring of stars', circular and ring-shaped spectra. 'Fractal' textures with '$1/f^P$'-type spectra

These two exercises deal with generating pseudo-random images using, in the DFT domain, spectral masks in the form of a 'ring of stars' (several spectral components uniformly arranged over the circumference of a circle of a certain radius centered at the DC component), in the form of circles and rings of certain radiuses and in the form of circularly symmetrical surfaces centered at the spectrum DC component that decay inversely proportionally to the 0.5th, first, 1.5th and second powers of the distance from the DC component ('$1/f^P$'-type spectra). The latter are sometimes called *'fractal' textures*.

For 'ring of stars' textures, the user is prompted to set the radius of a circle as a fraction of the image size, and the number of spectral components ('stars') uniformly arranged on the circumference of the circle. For textures with circular or ring-shaped spectra, the user-selected parameters are corresponding radiuses (in fractions of the image size). The programs can be run many times, producing different realizations of the textures with the same parameters. Examples of the resulting displays are presented in figures 6.5 and 6.6.

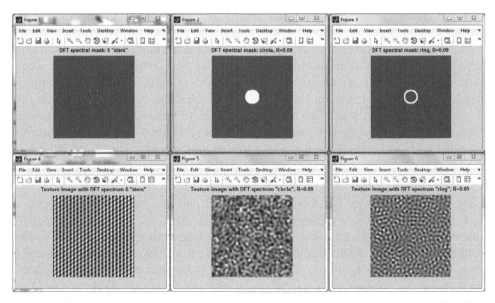

Figure 6.5. LF models: examples of generated images (bottom row) along with corresponding binary frequency responses of the linear filters applied to arrays of pseudo-random uncorrelated numbers as seed images. Yellow color in images of spectral masks corresponds to ones and blue color corresponds to zeros in the frequency responses.

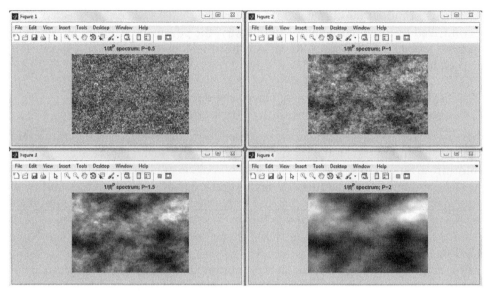

Figure 6.6. LF models: 'fractal' textures with circular power spectra that decay inversely proportional to powers 0.5, 1, 1.5 and 2 of the spatial frequency.

6.3.3 Imitation of natural textures

A remarkable property of LF models is their capability of imitating many types of natural texture. This can be done by assigning to arrays of pseudo-random images the power spectrum of a template texture image to be imitated. To demonstrate this capability, two options are offered in the exercise for selection of the template texture: (i) three types of natural texture are selected—a 'wood' texture of wooden furniture, a 'mohair' texture of woven woolen fabric and another texture, 'textile', of woven fabric, and (ii) an arbitrary image from the user's image database. The latter option is intended for the demonstration that not all natural texture can be imitated using the LF model. The program can be run many times to generate different realizations of texture images of the same type, which, in this case, is defined by the power spectrum of template natural texture images. Examples of outcomes are shown in figure 6.7.

6.3.4 Spatially inhomogeneous textures with controlled local spectra

In the previous exercise, LF models are applied globally, when global spectra of required textures are specified. Resulting textures are, therefore, spatially homogeneous (in terms of their local spectra). Local application of LF models enables generation of spatially inhomogeneous textures. For this, the specification of image local spectra is required. This can be done, for instance, using as a control signal an auxiliary image, whose local parameters determine the parameters of local spectra of the textures to be generated.

This idea is implemented in the exercise in the following way. Two types of spectral mask for the LF model are pre-defined: circular masks of different radii and elliptical masks of different orientations. For circular spectral masks, the mask radius is a

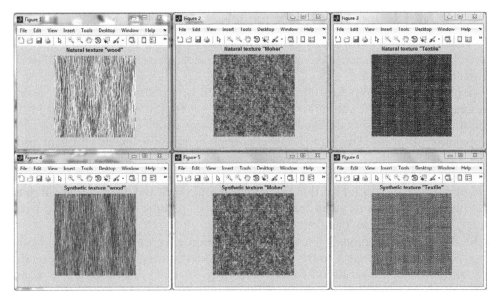

Figure 6.7. LF models: samples of natural textures (upper row) and their computer-generated imitations (lower row).

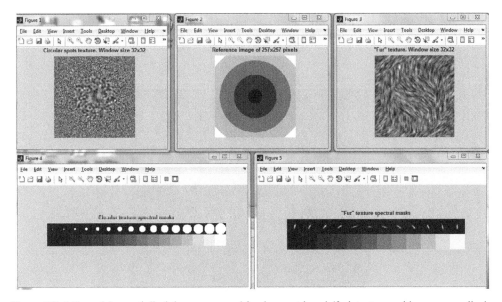

Figure 6.8. LF models: spatially inhomogeneous 'circular spots' and 'fur' textures with, correspondingly, circular and elliptical local spectra controlled by a reference image.

parameter controlled by the auxiliary image. For elliptical spectral masks, a controlled parameter is their angular orientation. In the process of texture image generation, these parameters are, pixel by pixel, determined by the gray levels of pixels of an auxiliary reference image selected by the user. Figure 6.8 illustrates the use of the model.

6.4 PWN&LF and LF&PWN models

PWN&LF and LF&PWN models are examples of two-stage models with point-wise nonlinearity and a linear filter applied to input seed images one after another in different orders.

A version of the PWN&LF model implemented here imitates 'randomly' tossing an image of a one cent coin onto a plane. To this goal, the model generates in the first stage an array of pseudo-random binary numbers with a certain, set by the user, probability of 'ones'. Then this array is convolved with an image of a cent coin, which plays here the role of the impulse response of the linear filter. As a result, images of cent coins are placed in the positions of the ones of the binary array at the filter input. The program runs this procedure several times and displays the obtained realizations of images as video frames. The number of runs is a user-defined parameter. Figure 6.9 shows one frame of such a run.

In the LF&WPN model, linear filters and point-wise nonlinearities act in the opposite order with respect to the previous case. First, arrays of correlated pseudo-random numbers are produced from a seed array of uncorrelated pseudo-random numbers by a linear filter with a preset frequency response, and then they are subjected, pixel by pixel, to a certain user-defined nonlinear transformation. The types of filter mask used here are the same as in the above-described exercise with the LF

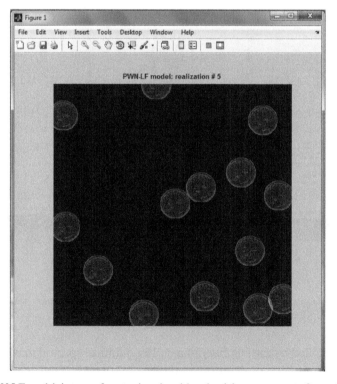

Figure 6.9. PWN&LF model: images of cent coins placed 'randomly' over an empty frame (shown using the MATLAB® colormap 'copper').

model. As for the nonlinearity, two options are offered: a threshold nonlinearity and a sinusoidal one. The threshold nonlinearity replaces positive input signal values by 'ones', and negative values by 'zeros'. The sinusoidal nonlinearity replaces input signal values by a cosine of 2π times the signal value normalized to unity. Figures 6.10 and 6.11 illustrate output displays.

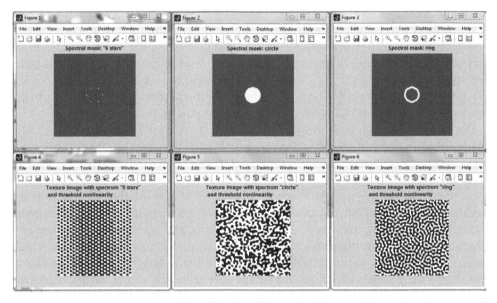

Figure 6.10. LF&PWN model: threshold nonlinearity. Yellow color in images of spectral masks corresponds to ones and blue color corresponds to zeros in the frequency responses.

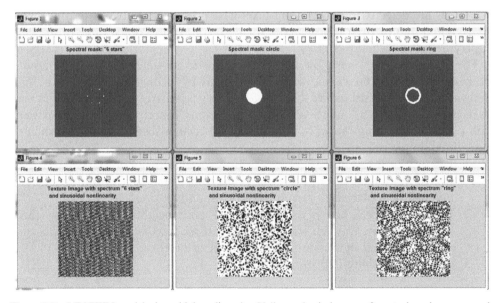

Figure 6.11. LF&PWN model: sinusoidal nonlinearity. Yellow color in images of spectral masks corresponds to ones and blue color corresponds to zeros in the filter frequency responses.

6.5 Evolutionary models

As mentioned, evolutionary models are models with feedback. They work in an iterative way, applying, at each iteration step, a certain image transformation specific for the model to the result obtained at the previous step. Two specific models are implemented here: a model that generates patchy patterns, and a model that generates maze-like patterns.

In the first model, images are iteratively subjected to a filter that works in a running (row-wise and column-wise) window and, at each position of the window, replaces the gray level of the window central pixel by the gray level of the mode of the histogram over the window, i.e. by the gray level most frequent in the window. This filter belongs to a family of rank filters that will be studied later in chapters 8 and 9. Being applied iteratively, it tends to produce piece-wise constant patchy patterns.

For experimentation with this model, the user is prompted first to select as a seed image either an array of pseudo-random uncorrelated numbers or any natural image from the image database, and then to set the filter window dimensions and the number of iterations. The program displays, at each iteration, the input seed image and the output image, and additionally the plots of the number of image pixels modified at each iteration and of the number of histogram bins in the output image versus the number of iterations. The first plot provides an indication of the convergence of the output image to a model 'fixed point', i.e. to a stable image, which, once it has appeared, is not modified anymore in the iteration process. The second plot shows the number of image histogram non-zero bins in the iteration process. Reduction of this number evidences the convergence of the seed image to a patchy piece-wise constant image. After the selected number of iterations is finished, the user has an option to display the pattern of edges of the produced patchy pattern. The edges are detected by computing pixel-wise differences between output image maxima and minima in a running window of 3×3 pixels. An example of the final display is shown in figure 6.12.

The second evolutionary model is a stochastic modification of the famous mathematical game the 'Game of Life', invented by British mathematician John Conway. In the standard model 'Game of Life', a square array of 'cells', which may be in one of two states, one ('live') and zero ('empty'), and form a binary pattern with pixels representing the cells, evolves from a certain seed pattern according to these three simple rules.

1. If a 'live' cell has in its closest 3×3 pixel spatial neighborhood fewer than two or more than three 'live' cells, it will 'die' at the next evolution step, i.e. one will be replaced by zero in the corresponding pixel.
2. If an 'empty' cell has in its closest 3×3 pixel neighborhood exactly three 'live' neighbors, this cell will give 'birth' at the next evolution step, i.e. zero will be replaced by one in the corresponding pixel.
3. Otherwise nothing happens.

The 'births' and 'deaths' events in the standard model happen at each evolution step in all cells of the array, where they must happen according to the above rules.

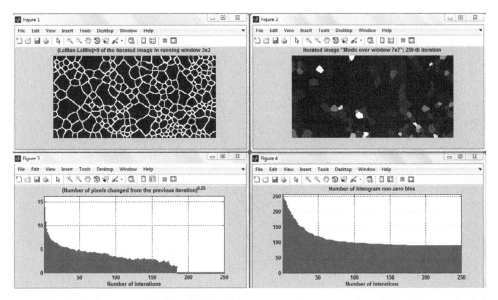

Figure 6.12. Evolutionary models: iterative local histogram modes over running window. The graph of the number of pixels changed from the previous iteration shows that the model reached its fixed point at about the 170th iteration.

In the stochastic modification of the model that is prepared for experimentation here, the 'birth' events occur in all cells where they should, whereas 'deaths' occur only in a subset of the relevant cells. Pixels of this subset are selected, using a pseudo-random number generator, with a certain probability, which we call the 'probability of death' P_{death}. This is a model parameter that the user has to set along with the initial probability of 'live' cells in the binary pseudo-random seed pattern that the program will generate at its start.

Obviously, for the standard model $P_{death} = 1$. The user can run the model with this parameter as well, but for P_{death} larger than about 0.3 the model does not seem to produce stable patterns however large the number of evolutionary steps. This becomes possible for lower values of P_{death}, and the model reaches, after a certain number of evolutionary steps, stable patterns, i.e. model fixed points, which turn out to be maze-like patterns of alternative straight vertical and horizontal lines, which chaotically switch their direction and/or positioning.

The simulation program displays, at each evolution step, the initial seed pattern, the output pattern and additionally a color coded output pattern, in which cells that are to 'die' on the next step are shown in red, cells that will give 'birth' are shown in green and stable cells are shown in blue. Displayed is also a plot of the relative number of cells that are to die. The plot serves as an indicator of the convergence of the pattern to a stable fixed point. Figure 6.13 illustrates an outcome of one of the runs of the simulation program. It shows that the complete stabilization of the pattern took about 15 000 evolution steps. Generally, this number varies very substantially for different realizations of pseudo-random seed patterns.

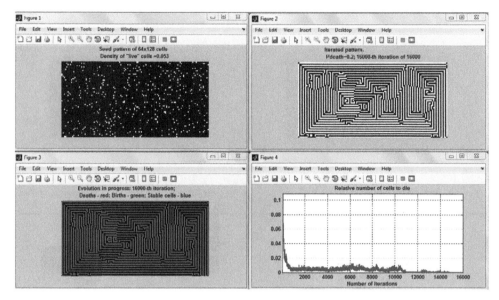

Figure 6.13. Evolutionary models: stochastic modification of the 'Game of Life'. The bottom image and plot evidence that the model reached a fixed point after about 15 000 iterations.

6.6 Questions for self-testing

1. What is the principle of the algorithmic approach to models for generating patterns with prescribed statistical characteristics?
2. Which statistical characteristics of images are controlled by PWN and LF models?
3. How can PWN and LF models be used for imitating different types of image noise?
4. Do 'fractal' textures with $1/f^P$-type spectra and spatially inhomogeneous textures generated by LF models resemble any natural textures?
5. Does the appearance of textures generated with the use of LF models resemble the shape of filter masks of the models?
6. What kinds of natural texture can be imitated by the LF models and what cannot?
7. Define, in terms of the algorithmic approach, the model that produces 'random net' patterns such as patterns of edges of patchy piece-wise constant images.
8. Do maze-like patterns generated by the evolutionary 'Game of Life'-based model resemble some natural patterns?
9. Suggest some other multi-level algorithmic models as an extension of those implemented in the exercises.

IOP Publishing

Advanced Digital Imaging Laboratory Using MATLAB®

Leonid P Yaroslavsky

Chapter 7

Image correlators for detection and localization of objects

7.1 Introduction

Object detection and localization is one of the basic tasks in image processing. Obviously, solving this task assumes the availability of a template image of the sought target object and requires one method or another of numerical evaluation of the similarity between the template image and fragments of observed images in which the presence of the target object is expected. If the image contains, in some place, a precise copy of the target template, any reasonable similarity measure can be used for target detection equally successfully. This, however, never happens: images of target objects are never precise copies of their templates. The fundamental reason for that is the presence of random noise in observed images. Other image distortions are also possible. In the presence of noise, no method is capable of unerring detection and localization of objects. Therefore one should find optimal methods that secure the most reliable detection and accurate localization of targets in the presence of image distortions and noise.

For the case when an image containing a target object has an empty background and the only obstacle for target localization is contamination of the image by additive signal independent uncorrelated Gaussian noise, the optimal method for target detection and localization is known. It consists in computing image correlations with the target object template and location coordinates of the correlation maximum, which are the statistically best possible estimate of the target object position within the image. This process is also called 'matched filtering', and the image correlator that implements it is called the *matched filter correlator*.

There are a number of real applications in which such a model of target localization in images with signal independent uncorrelated Gaussian noise is adequate. A typical example is navigation in space using images of stars. The importance of this model is also associated with the fact that it is a special case of the more fundamental and

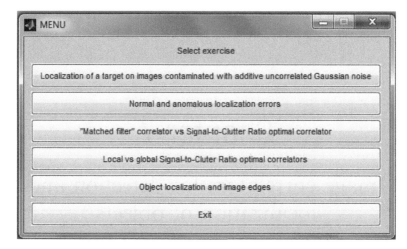

Figure 7.1. Entrance menu 'Image correlators for detection and localization of objects'.

general problem of parameter estimation in images, for which it gives an example of the existence of an optimal and ultimate solution.

However, in a much larger number of applications such a model is too simplistic. First of all, the assumption of empty background does not hold often. The background images either contain a number of non-overlapping non-target objects, as for instance, in the case of character recognition in text, or, even worse, contain clutters of overlapping non-target objects, which can be easily confused with the target under search.

The exercises in this chapter are targeted at studying the performance of the standard matched filter image correlator in different circumstances and its adaptive modifications optimized for reliable target detection in cluttered images. The exercises are listed in the entrance menu of this chapter, shown in figure 7.1.

7.2 Localization of a target on images contaminated with additive uncorrelated Gaussian noise. Normal and anomalous localization errors

This section contains exercises that simulate the matched filter correlator for localization of target objects in images contaminated by additive signal independent uncorrelated Gaussian noise and demonstrate its performance in terms of *localization accuracy and reliability*. It includes three exercises.

For the exercise 'Localization of a target on empty background', two test target objects are prepared, 'constellation' and 'character "o"', which have different signal energies (sum of squared pixel gray values). The exercise demonstrates, by visualizing results of localization experiments with several realizations of additive uncorrelated Gaussian noise, that when the noise level is sufficiently low the matched filter correlator detects the target in a close vicinity of its actual position, whereas when the noise level is sufficiently high it frequently happens that the matched

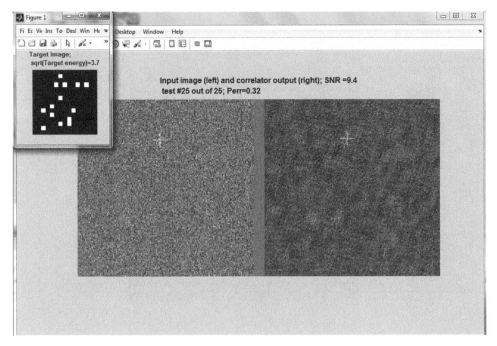

Figure 7.2. Localization of a target image 'constellation' on empty background contaminated with additive signal independent uncorrelated Gaussian noise. The cross symbol indicates the position of the target in the image (left image) and the result its location in the position of the highest maximum in the correlation plane (right image).

filter correlator misses the target and erroneously finds its coordinates far away from the target's actual position. The noise intensity and the number of realizations are user-selected parameters. An example of the experiment's outcome is given in figure 7.2. Displayed are, along with the result of localization, signal-to-noise ratio, the number of noise realizations and the relative number of false detections (probability of error P_{err}). The two prepared target objects have different energies. This enables comparison of the probability of errors for them for the same intensity of noise.

This exercise is supplemented with the exercise 'Localization of a character in text', which demonstrates that the probability of wrong localization of the target object rises, for the same noise level, substantially if the image contains non-target objects with which the target object might be confused. The experiment runs for several numbers of noise realizations, and the user can see how frequently this confusion happens and what characters are most frequently confused with the test character. The number of noise realizations and intensity of additive noise are user-selected parameters in this experiment too. Figure 7.3 shows an example of one of the experiment's runs. Displayed are the results of localization, signal-to-noise ratio and the number of noise realizations.

A fundamental phenomenon in target detection in additive Gaussian noise is the threshold effect: if the signal-to-noise ratio (SNR) falls below a certain threshold level, the probability of erroneous target localization far from its actual position P_{err}

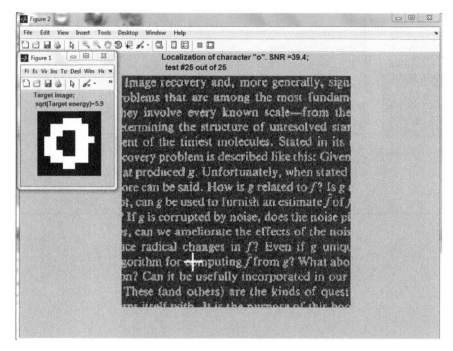

Figure 7.3. Localization of a character in text. The detected character is marked by the cross.

rises, with the decrease of SNR, very rapidly to one. The speed of growth tends to infinity with the number Q of possible positions of the target object within the image (it is roughly equal to the ratio of the area of search to the area occupied by the target object). The theoretical value of the threshold is defined by the equation

$$2\sigma_n^2 \ln Q/E_{tgt} = 1 \qquad (7.1)$$

where σ_n^2 is the variance of the additive noise and E_{tgt} is the target image energy (the sum of squared pixel gray values).

This phenomenon is demonstrated in the exercise 'Threshold effect in the probability of target detection error'. The program that implements the exercise runs a user-selected number of iterations of detection of a test object (a square of 8×8 pixels) on an empty background of four sizes (64×64, 128×128, 256×256 and 512×512 pixels, which corresponds to $Q = 64$, 256, 1024 and 4096) for nine preset levels of noise, and estimates, upon completion of the iterations, the probability of detection errors. Results of the detection are qualified as wrong if the localization error exceeds the target object dimensions, 8 pixels. Typical curves of the probability of false detection as functions of noise-to-signal ratio for different Q obtained in the exercise are presented in figure 7.4.

Full statistical characterization of target localization errors is provided by the localization error distribution density. It can be experimentally evaluated in the exercise 'Normal and anomalous localization errors'. The program simulates localization of an impulse observed in additive signal independent uncorrelated Gaussian noise of

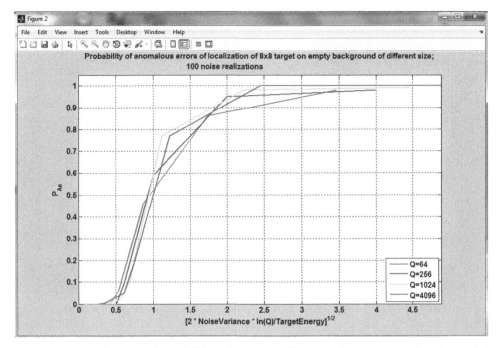

Figure 7.4. Threshold effect in the probability of target detection error. Q means the number of potentially possible positions of the target with the field of search.

different levels, and runs, for each specific level of noise, a number of iterations with different realizations of noise. Upon completion of the iterations, a distribution histogram of localization errors observed in all iterations as well as their variance is evaluated. For each level of noise, the program plots the test impulse and its mixture with noise, the distribution functions of localization errors (i.e. differences between the actual impulse position and its estimations by the matched filter correlator) and, additionally, estimates of the localization error variance. The latter is plotted along with its theoretical values, which are obtained in the assumption of low noise level. At the start of the experiment, the user is prompted to set the width (in number of samples) of the test impulse of Gaussian shape, the start value of the standard deviation of noise, the number N_{nsr} of noise levels to be tested and increments of this value (DELTA$_{nsr}$) as well as the number N_{iter} of noise realizations to be tested for each noise level. An example of the final display is presented in figure 7.5.

7.3 'Matched filter' correlator versus signal-to-clutter ratio optimal correlator and local versus global signal-to-clutter ratio optimal correlators

The matched filter correlator, being optimal for target location in uncorrelated additive noise, in most applications, when targets should be detected and located in images that contain cluttered background, shows a very high rate of false alarms.

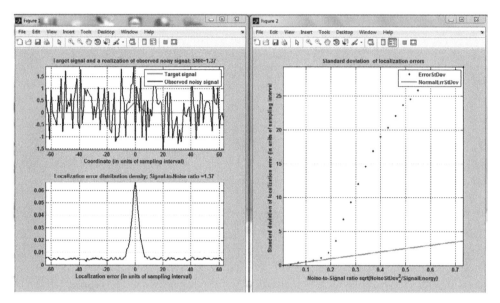

Figure 7.5. Output display of the exercise 'Normal and anomalous localization errors'.

A simple modification of the matched filter correlator called the *optimal adaptive correlator*, or *signal-to-clutter ratio (SCR) optimal correlator*, substantially improves its discrimination capability. In a distinction from the matched filter correlator, whose frequency response is just a complex conjugate to the target image Fourier spectrum, in the frequency response of the SCR optimal correlator the complex conjugate to target image Fourier spectrum is divided by an estimate of the power spectrum of the background image component that does not contain the target, or, in the assumption that the target occupies a small portion of the image, by the power spectrum of the entire image. This modification secures in the SCR optimal correlator output the highest ratio of the signal value in the target location position to the signal standard deviation over the non-target background part of the image and makes the correlator adaptive to images in which the target is sought.

The first exercise in this group implements localization of a fragment of one of two stereo images in the second image. At the start, the user is prompted to choose, using a cross symbol, a position on the displayed image of its fragment to be detected. Then a panel is opened to select the size, in pixels, of the fragment (target size). The larger the size, the better the reliability of target detection. Once the target size is selected, the program displays the results of localization of the selected fragment by the matched filter correlator and by the SCR optimal correlator, with detected locations being indicated by crosses in corresponding images, outputs of both correlators presented by gray levels of pixels of the correlation images, and plots of rows of the corresponding correlator outputs. On the latter, ratios of the signal maxima at the target location to the standard deviation of the corresponding correlator outputs are also provided in titles to plots. The experiment can be repeated with another image fragment as a target. Figure 7.6 represents an example of the program output.

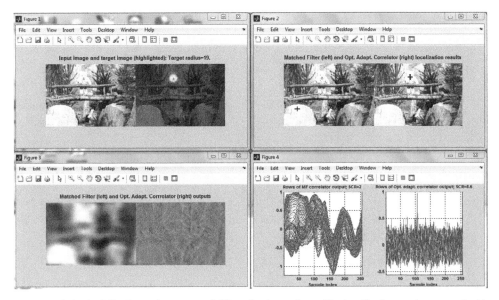

Figure 7.6. 'Matched filter' correlator versus SCR optimal correlator. The localization results are marked by crosses. The sharp peak in the plots of rows of output of the SCR optimal correlator indicates the position of the target.

Thanks to the fact that frequency responses of SCR optimal correlators depend on both target image and input image spectra, SCR optimal correlators are adaptive to images, i.e. to image background components, against which the target image should be discriminated.

Obviously, the adaptation will be more efficient for images that are more homogeneous in the spatial distribution of objects and their shapes and sizes, i.e. are more homogeneous in terms of 'local' spectra. Therefore, one may expect that the discrimination capability of SCR optimal correlators will be better if they are applied locally to individual image fragments that contain smaller numbers of non-target objects. In order to perform the search over the entire image frame, one should implement the SCR optimal correlator in a window scanning the image pixel by pixel and measure the correlator outputs at all positions of the window. The decision on the location of the searched target should be taken upon localization of the global maximum of the correlator outputs.

The local adaptive SCR optimal correlators are implemented in the exercise 'Local versus global signal-to-clutter ratio optimal correlators', which are targeted at a comparison of the discrimination capabilities of the global and SCR optimal correlators. As test images, the same pair of stereoscopic images as in the previous exercise is suggested to be used, and the exercise is performed in the same way. For the local SCR optimal correlator, dimensions of the scanning search window are taken as five times the target dimensions. Displayed are two test images, outputs of the SCR optimal correlator in the process of scanning and, upon completion of scanning of the entire image, the results of target detection by SCR-optimal correlators in both global and local applications. As a numerical measure of the correlators'

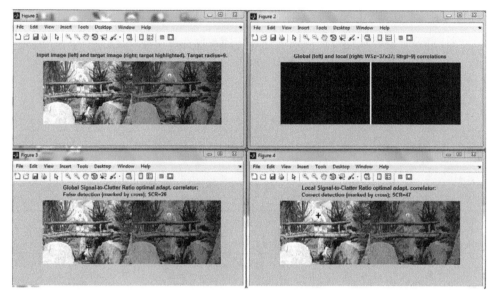

Figure 7.7. Output display in the exercise 'Local versus global signal-to-clutter ratio optimal correlators'.

discrimination capability, 'signal-to-clutter' ratios are given in the titles of the output images. Figure 7.7 illustrates one of the outcomes of the exercise.

7.4 Object localization and image edges

Exercises of this group are intended to provide a deeper insight into the use of SCR optimal correlators. As frequency responses of SCR optimal correlators are the ratio $(Sp_{tgt})^*/|Sp_{img}|^2$ of the complex conjugate to the target image spectrum $(Sp_{tgt})^*$ to the image power spectrum $|Sp_{img}|^2$, their operation can be treated as a two-step image filtering: first by the filter with frequency response $1/|Sp_{img}|$ and then by the filter with frequency response $(Sp_{tgt})^*/|Sp_{img}|$. The first filter makes the amplitude of the spectrum of the input image uniform (similarly to the uniform spectrum of white light). It is called a '*whitening*' *filter*. The second filter is, obviously, the filter matched to the 'whitened' target object modified by the first filter. This means that SCR optimal correlators can be treated as matched filter correlators for 'whitened' input and target images.

Intensities of spectral components of images usually more or less rapidly decay with frequency. Therefore, whitening filters correspondingly amplify high-frequency image components. In images that contain sets of objects separated by object borders, image whitening results in what can be called *edge enhancement*. The first exercise in this group, 'Image whitening', demonstrates such an edge enhancement on test images selected by the user. Along with whitening, test images are also subjected, for comparison, to the well known method of edge extraction, filtering using the 2D '*Laplacian*' *operator* with 2D point spread function, in MATLAB® denotations, $[-0.1 \ -0.15 \ -0.1; \ -0.15 \ 1 \ -0.15; \ -0.1 \ -0.15 \ -0.1]$. In addition, local means in the window of 9×9 pixels over the squared modulus of the whitened image

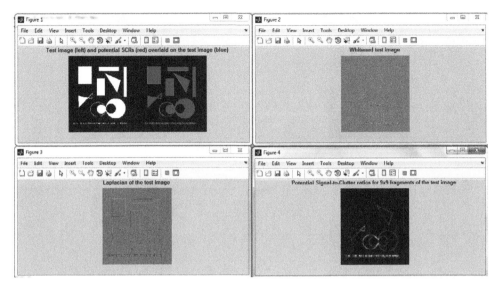

Figure 7.8. Object localization and image edges: image whitening and Laplacian.

are computed. Theoretically, they represent, for all pixels, potential signal-to-clutter ratios at the output of the SCR optimal correlator for 9×9 pixel image fragments centered at these pixels, if they were used as target objects. These ratios characterize the potential 'goodness' of these fragments for their localization in the given image. The results are displayed as illustrated in figure 7.8.

Comparison of matched filter correlator and SCR optimal correlators evidences that image whitening, that makes the image spectrum amplitude uniform, is a key reason for the improved discrimination capability of SCR optimal correlators. In whitened images, only the spectrum phase component of the initial image spectrum is kept. This tells us that the phase component of image spectra contains all the information needed for the recognition of image objects.

The second exercise in this group, 'Exchange of spectra amplitude components between two images', provides an opportunity to check this property of images. As a test pair of images, images 'Mona Lisa' and 'Barbara' are suggested. The user also has an option to use any other pair of images from his/her image database. The program displays the selected images and copies of these images in which image power spectra are exchanged. Figure 7.9 illustrates the result. Note that it is recommended to experiment with different test images, those that contain individual objects and images that do not contain any individual objects (i.e. textures).

7.5 Questions for self-testing

1. In the experiment on target localization, does the matched filter correlator perform similarly for the two test targets for the same noise level?
2. In experiments on the detection of a character in text, what other characters are most frequently confused with the test character 'o' and why?

Figure 7.9. Exchange of spectra amplitude components between two images: a result for 'Mona Lisa' and 'Barbara' test images.

3. Can you distinguish in the localization error distribution density areas that correspond to normal (small) and anomalous (large) localization errors? Why are the tails of the distribution density for large noise levels uniform?

4. How can the substantial increase of the localization error variances from their theoretical estimates for a sufficiently large level of noise be explained?

5. Using the results of the comparison of the matched filter and SCR optimal correlators, how can one explain the variability of the results for different image fragments as target objects?

6. In the experiment on image whitening with the test image 'geometrical figures' illustrated in figure 7.8, some characters promise, according to the map of potential SCRs, substantially larger SCRs than others. How can one explain this?

7. Why are the vertical and horizontal edges of rectangles in the test image 'geometrical figures' shown in figure 7.8 not enhanced in the whitened image as much as the edges of the other figures? Which features of the test figures are most enhanced and why?

8. What conclusion can be derived from the similarity and dissimilarity between whitened images and their Laplacians?

9. What is the rational explanation of a common belief that edge enhancement and extraction is useful for recognizing images?

10. Is it true for all types of image that the phase rather than the amplitude components of image spectra carry information needed for image identification?

IOP Publishing

Advanced Digital Imaging Laboratory Using MATLAB®

Leonid P Yaroslavsky

Chapter 8

Methods of image perfecting

8.1 Introduction

Image perfecting is a primary task of image processing. It is aimed at producing, from raw images generated by real imperfect imaging systems, images that would be produced by perfect systems, i.e. images without, as far as it is possible, distortions, which appear in raw images due to degradations in imaging systems. Typical image degradations in real imaging systems are

- degradations due to nonlinearity of the system *gray scale transfer functions*, which ideally must be linear within the image dynamic range
- image blur due to imperfection of the imaging system *frequency transfer functions*, which ideally must be uniform in the image base band
- degradations due to various imaging system random noises.

Exercises in this chapter are designed for practicing with methods of correction of these typical image degradations. They are listed in the entrance menu shown in figure 8.1.

8.2 Correcting imaging system transfer functions

This section contains exercises on correction of the imaging system gray scale transfer function, both known and unknown, and correction of the imaging system frequency transfer function. They implement a straightforward approach of *inverse filtering*; i.e. image distortions are corrected by means of applying to distorted images a transformation inverse to that which caused the distortions. This approach works if the noise level in the image signals is sufficiently low.

The first exercise in this section, 'Correction of imaging system gray scale transfer function', demonstrates this 'inverse filtering' method for correcting known and unknown gray scale transfer functions.

In the case of a known imaging system gray scale transfer function, the correcting inverse gray scale transformation is implemented explicitly and is applied to test

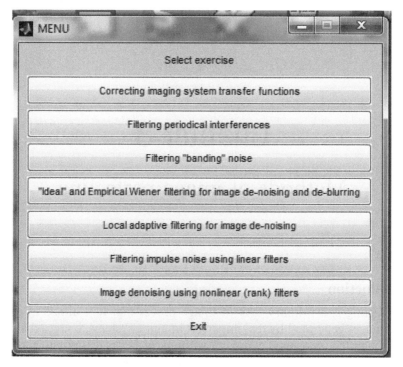

Figure 8.1. Methods of image perfection: the entrance menu.

images distorted by a *P*-law nonlinear transformation and quantization to 256 gray
levels simulated according to the equation

$$\text{INPIMG\_NL} = \text{round}(128*(1 + \text{sign}(\text{INPIMG} - 128).$$
$$*\text{abs}(\text{INPIMG}/128 - 1).\,{}^{\wedge}P)) \qquad (8.1)$$

where INPIMG and INPIMG_NL are the non-distorted test image and distorted
image, respectively both with quantized gray scale values in the range [0–255]. For
experimentation, the user can select either a prepared test image, 'face', or any other
test image from his/her image database. The simulation program prompts the user to
specify the *P* parameter of the *P*-law nonlinear transformation and the noise level in
the distorted image (in terms of the PSNR of the image dynamic range 256 to the
standard deviation of normal additive noise) and displays the initial non-distorted
image, the distribution histogram of its gray levels, the distorted image, plots of
distortion and correction functions and the output corrected image and its histogram.
An illustrative example is shown in figure 8.2. As an option, the program displays, in
place of plots of distortion and correcting functions, the difference between initial and
corrected images (correction error), in order to enable visual and quantitative (in
terms of the restoration error standard deviation) evaluation of the correction quality.

For correcting distortions caused by an unknown imaging system gray scale
transfer function, one can use a method of '*standardization*' *of image histograms*, i.e. of
converting the distorted image into an image with a certain particular histogram,

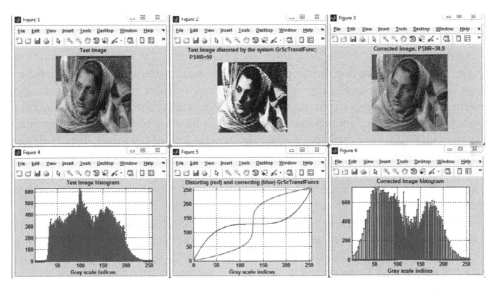

Figure 8.2. Correction of known imaging system gray scale transfer function by means of applying a correcting transfer function inverse to the distortion function.

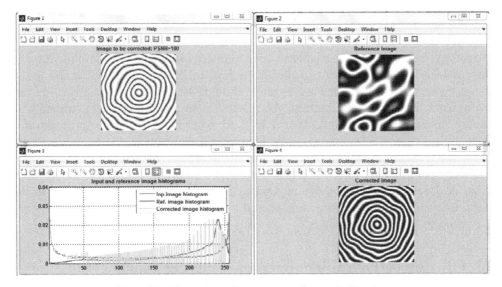

Figure 8.3. Correcting unknown gray scale transfer function.

typical for the family of images to which the given image belongs. As a reference histogram, the histogram of a reference 'standard' image can be used. In the exercise, this option is illustrated on an example of correcting the unknown g distortion of an interferogram. As a reference image, a simulated good quality interferogram is used. The program prompts the user to specify the noise level (PSNR) in the distorted image and displays the distorted image, reference image, corrected image and plots of histograms of the distorted and reference images, as illustrated in figure 8.3.

Optionally, the user can also use for experiments any other pair of images from the user's database, the first of which is regarded as a 'distorted' image and the second as a reference image.

The second exercise is correcting the imaging system frequency transfer function using the 'inverse filtering' approach. The frequency transfer function of the imaging system to be corrected is supposed to known. Specifically, the exercise is designed to correct degradations of image sharpness due to finite sizes of apertures of the image sensor, such as a scanner or a photographic camera, and of the image display device. Frequency transfer functions of image sensors and display devices are Fourier transforms of their aperture functions. The overall frequency responses of imaging systems that consist of image sensors and display devices are a product of those frequency responses.

The exercise is designed in the assumption that sensor and display apertures have a square shape with size equal to the distance between pixels in the sensor, and, correspondingly, in the display devices multiplied by a corresponding shape factor, whose value is less than one. The larger the shape factors the more severe are the image sharpness degradations due to weakening of the image high-frequency spectral components in image sensor and display devices.

The frequency response of the *inverse filter* that corrects these distortions is inversely proportional to the product of the frequency responses of the image sensor and display devices. For frequencies where sensor and display device frequency responses are equal to zero (or, generally, are smaller than a certain threshold), the correcting frequency response is set to zero in order to prevent overamplification of noise, which is always present in the image and otherwise is negligible. As a test image, a prepared 'face' image is suggested, though the user can select any other test image from his/her image database. The user is also prompted to set camera and display shape factors and noise level PSNR to experiment with. The program displays input and corrected images and, as an additional option, the imaging system frequency response for visual evaluation of the degree of weakening of image high-frequency components in the imaging system. In addition, the difference between initial and corrected images, which represents an image component added to the initial image for its correction, is displayed as well. These two output displays are illustrated in figures 8.4 and 8.5.

8.3 Filtering periodical interferences. Filtering 'banding' noise

Noise in imaging systems is a fundamental factor that puts limits on image suitability for analysis and on possibilities of correcting other image distortions. In cases when noise cannot be tolerated, image denoising is required. There are many methods of image denoising, linear and nonlinear filtering ones, aimed at different types of noise. Exercises in this section demonstrate denoising images distorted by so-called *narrow-band noise*. Specifically, linear filtering methods for image cleaning from periodical interferences and *banding noise* are dealt with. In chapter 5, methods for diagnostics of parameters on these types of noise were demonstrated. These methods are used in denoising.

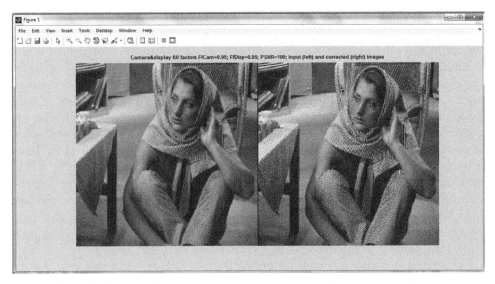

Figure 8.4. Correcting imaging system frequency response: initial and corrected images.

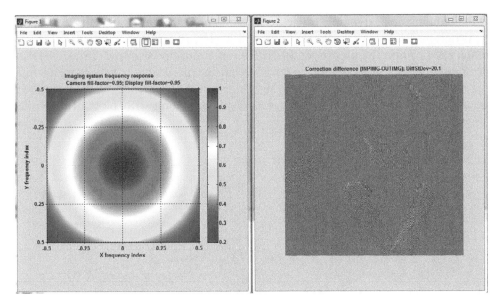

Figure 8.5. Correcting imaging system frequency response: an imaging system frequency response (shown as an image in pseudo-colors coded according to the color bar) and a correcting image component added to the initial image to correct its sharpness degradations.

Theoretically, using linear filtering for image denoising is based on the ideas of *empirical Wiener filtering*. Although, generally, the capability of Wiener filtering for image cleaning from additive noise has certain limitations, as will be demonstrated later in the exercises of this chapter, in its application to cleaning narrow-band noise empirical Wiener filtering proved to be very efficient.

The first exercise in this set of exercises demonstrates *rejection empirical Wiener filtering* of *periodical noise* (*moiré noise*), which contains only a few isolated components in the DFT, DCT, Walsh or other transform spectra. For detecting and evaluating the intensity of these components, methods of noise diagnostics demonstrated in chapter 5 are used. In rejection filtering, the detected noise components are completely eliminated. Two implementations of rejection moiré noise filtering are offered: filtering in DFT and filtering in DCT domains. As a test image, two prepared images with real (not simulated) noise are suggested in the exercise; the use of another image from the user's image database is possible as well. Upon selecting a test image, a plot of row-wise averaged DFT, or, correspondingly, a DCT power spectrum of image rows is displayed, and the user is prompted to set a threshold for detecting noise peaks. Once the detection threshold is set, the program displays the result of the filtering, the difference between initial and filtered images and the averaged power spectrum of filtered image rows along with that of the initial image. An example of the final display is presented in figure 8.6.

The second exercise is image cleaning from 'banding' interferences. As test images, three options are suggested: simulated banding noise and two images with real, not simulated banding interferences. In the case of 'simulated banding noise', the user is prompted to load a test image from the user's image database and then to set the banding noise dynamic range (as a fraction of the image range [0–255]). Then the program displays the noised image and a plot, in another window, of its row means and prompts the user to set the size of the smoothing window that will be used for smoothing the sequence of row-wise local means, using 1D local mean filter (see chapter 5), for subsequent detection of noise outbursts. Once the window size is specified, the resulting denoised image is displayed along with plots of smoothed

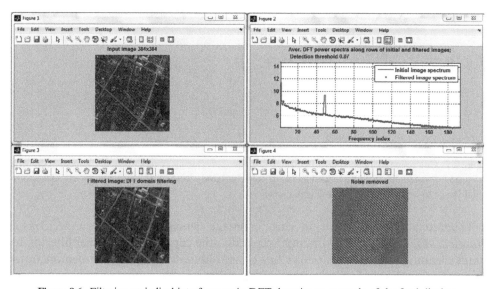

Figure 8.6. Filtering periodical interferences in DFT domain: an example of the final display.

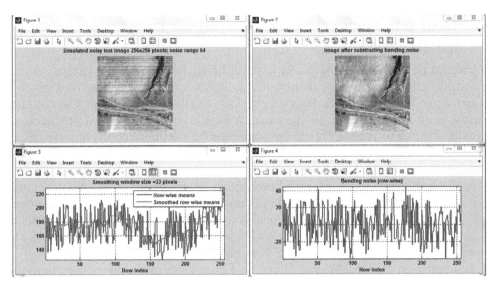

Figure 8.7. Filtering banding noise: simulated interference.

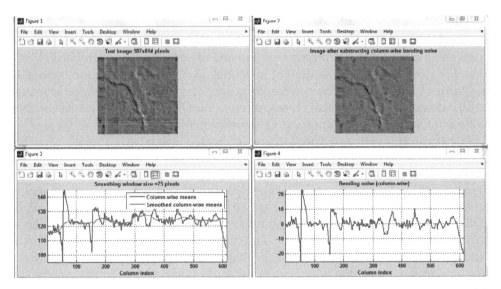

Figure 8.8. Filtering banding noise: real image. Shown is the result of the second pass (column-wise) of the filtering.

image row means and of the difference between initial and smoothed row means, which represents removed banding noise (see figure 8.7).

When one of two images with real banding noise is selected for testing, the user has to only select the size of the row means smoothing window. Note that the test image 'Mars satellite image' is distorted by two types of banding noise: row-wise and column-wise. Therefore, noise cleaning is performed in this case in two passes: row-wise cleaning and then column-wise cleaning. The resulting display is shown in figure 8.8.

8.4 'Ideal' and empirical Wiener filtering for image denoising and deblurring

Theoretically, Wiener filtering can be used for both noise cleaning and for correcting image blur originated from weakening image high-frequency components in imaging systems. As was mentioned, Wiener filtering is sufficiently efficient for cleaning narrow-band additive noise, but has quite a limited capability of cleaning additive broadband noise in images. Due to the noise present, the image deblurring capability of Wiener filtering is also limited. Exercises in this section are designed for experimental study of these limitations.

In the first exercise, the image deblurring/denoising capabilities of the ideal and empirical Wiener filters are compared in terms of usability for reading of a test image 'text' restored by the filters from its noisy and blurred original for different levels of noise and different degrees of blur. Both image noising by additive uncorrelated noise and image blur by a 'Gaussian' blur function are simulated.

To implement the ideal Wiener filter, exact knowledge of the power spectra of the realization of noise and of the noise free image are required. Though these data are in reality not available, in computer simulation realizations of noise and non-distorted signal, and therefore their power spectra, are known.

The empirical Wiener filter is the Wiener filter in which the power spectrum of the noiseless image is estimated as a difference between the power spectrum of the distorted image and a constant that represents an estimate of variance of uncorrelated (white) noise. Because particular realizations of noise may have variances not exactly equal to the statistical variance and their power spectra are not uniform, it is common to set, for the filter design, the constant that represents noise variance equal to the statistical noise variance multiplied by a certain noise variance estimation factor of the range [1–2].

For experimentation, a prepared test image 'text' is suggested, although any other image from the user's image data set can be used. Before running the program, the user is prompted to select, from the displayed menu, a blur factor and peak signal-to-noise ratio (PSNR). Blur factor is a value that, roughly, is inversely proportional to the width of the Gaussian frequency response of the image blurring filter that will be applied to the test image in order to simulate its blur. There is a 'no blur' option in the menu as well. The PSNR is the ratio of the image range maximum to the standard deviation of uncorrelated noise that is added to the blurred image. Once these settings are made, the difference between the initial and distorted images and the image restored by the 'ideal Wiener' filter are displayed, along with the difference between the initial and restored images (ideal Wiener filter restoration error), for visual evaluation. Then the user is prompted to set the noise variance estimation factor, after which the image restored by the empirical Wiener filter is displayed along with the empirical Wiener filter restoration error. If the empirical Wiener filtering restoration result is not satisfactory, another, usually larger, noise variance estimation factor should be set. An illustrative final display is presented in figure 8.9.

The second exercise, 'Inspection of potentials of image restoration capability of the ideal and empirical Wiener filters', is aimed at quantitative evaluation of the image restoration capability limits of the 'ideal' and empirical Wiener filters. To this goal, for

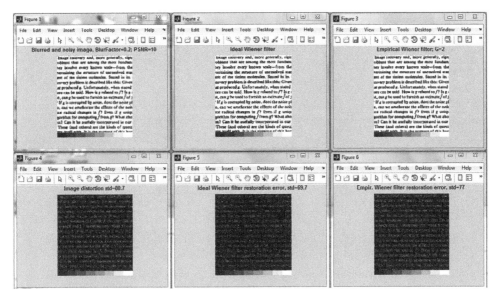

Figure 8.9. Examples of image denoising and deblurring by the 'ideal' and empirical Wiener filters (parameter 'std' denotes standard deviation of corresponding difference images).

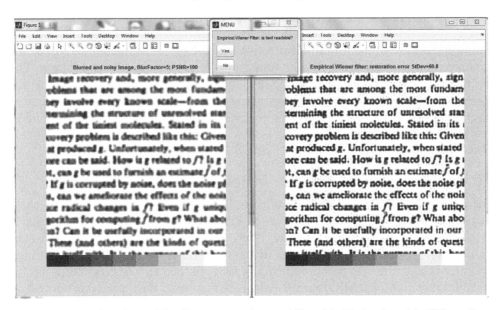

Figure 8.10. Inspection of potentials of image restoration capability of the ideal and empirical Wiener filters: one of the intermediate displays.

each particular PSNR from the set of values [1, 2, 3, 5, 10, 20, 30, 40, 50, 100], the image is subjected to blur with different blur factors, one by one, and then the image distorted in this way is restored, first by the ideal and second by the 'empirical' Wiener filter. Results are displayed one after another, and the user has to decide whether the restored image is readable. One of the intermediate displays is shown in figure 8.10.

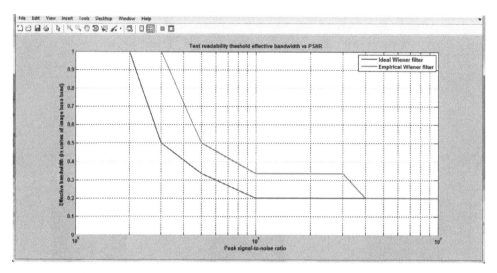

Figure 8.11. Inspection of potentials of image restoration capability of the ideal and empirical Wiener filters: final plots of the restoration capability thresholds.

Once an acceptable restoration result is confirmed by the user, the corresponding blur factor and PSNR are stored and the experiment is repeated for the next level of PSNR. As soon as all values of PSNR have been tested for all blur factors, the program plots the stored 'threshold effective bandwidth', corresponding to used blur factors versus respective PSNRs for both 'ideal' and empirical Wiener filters. The meaning of these plots is simple: for pairs 'effective bandwidth' and 'PSNR' which correspond to points above the corresponding curves, the filters restore the degraded image satisfactorily; for pairs 'effective bandwidth' and 'PSNR' which correspond to points beneath the curves, the filters are not able to restore the images. An exemplar of such 'threshold' plots is shown in figure 8.11.

8.5 Local adaptive filtering for image denoising

The noise suppressing capability of Wiener filters has its roots in the energy compaction capability of the transforms, which was studied in the exercises of chapter 2. In the previous exercises in this chapter, Wiener filtering was applied 'globally', i.e. to entire image frames. However, images that contain sets of isolated objects separated by object borders are very inhomogeneous in terms of their local spectra: local spectra of sufficiently small image fragments, which, at the same time, are large enough to contain at least one object, vary very substantially from one fragment to another. The exercise 'Image power spectra' in chapter 5 demonstrates this phenomenon. Therefore, to make full use of the transform energy compaction property, one should apply Wiener filtering to image individual fragments rather than globally. Such filtering will obviously be locally adaptive as filter frequency responses will be built on the basis of estimation of the image local spectra in each window position.

Exercises in this section implement this idea of local adaptive empirical Wiener filtering in a running window. The first exercise demonstrates local adaptive filtering for denoising 1D signals. As test signals, two options are offered: computer-generated pseudo-random piece-wise constant signals and a sample electrocardiogram. Filter implementation in two transform domains, Haar and discrete cosine transforms, can be tested. Implemented are *'rejective' filters*, that set transform coefficients which are below a certain filtering threshold to zero and do not modify any other coefficients. For experimentation, the user is prompted to select the transform and specify the noise level (in the units of the signal range), filter window size (in the case of work in the Haar transform domain window size must be an integer power of two) and filtering threshold. The latter is an empirical estimate of additive noise standard deviation and, therefore, has to be of the same order of magnitude.

Once parameters are set, the program displays results in four subplots as exemplified in figure 8.12. The first subplot is the test signal with added noise. The second subplot is an image whose columns present, for each position of the sliding window central sample, local transform spectra with intensities of spectral coefficients represented by gray levels of the corresponding pixels. The third subplot is the same spectral image after thresholding. These two subplots are what is called *'time–frequency' signal representation*. The fourth subplot shows the output filtered signal. The user has a possibility to visually evaluate the filtering quality and try to achieve a better result by changing filter parameters, window size and filtering threshold.

The second exercise deals with testing 2D local adaptive DCT domain filtering. 2D *local adaptive linear filtering* is performed by means of scanning the input image row-wise/column-wise with a moving window. At each window position, an estimate of the central pixel of the window is produced, using either the empirical Wiener or rejective filter designed in the DCT domain for the image fragment within the window. In such a way, the output image is generated pixel by pixel.

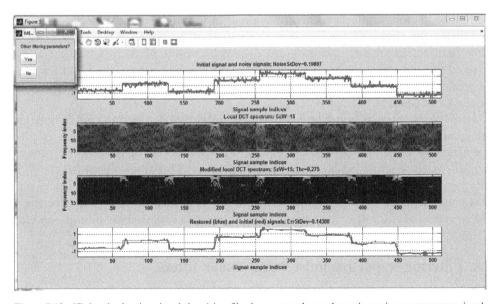

Figure 8.12. 1D local adaptive signal denoising filtering: a pseudo-random piece-wise constant test signal.

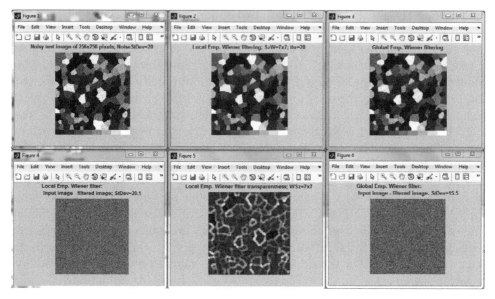

Figure 8.13. An example of 2D local adaptive image denoising filtering: piece-wise constant test image.

For exercises, a prepared piece-wise constant test image or any other image from the user's image database can be used as a test image. The use of the piece-wise constant test image enables better evaluation of the edge preservation capability of local adaptive filters.

At the program start, it prompts the user to set the standard deviation of noise (in units of image gray levels) to be added to the selected test image, displays the noised image and then prompts the setting of the filter window size and the noise variance estimation factor, similarly to how it is done in the first exercise (global filtering), and finally the choice of the filter type ('rejective' or 'empirical Wiener' filter). Once filter parameters are set, the program displays a result of the application of the selected filter to the entire test image and the difference between the input noiseless image and filtered noisy image and starts local filtering. Results of local filtering are displayed in the real time of processing.

Displayed are the output filtered image, the difference between the initial noiseless image and the noisy image and an image isomorphic map of the number of filter frequency response non-zero coefficients in the window (as fractions of the window size) for each window position in the scan process. This fraction, called the *filter transparentness*, is a value between zero and one, and is encoded, for display purposes, as image gray levels. Figure 8.13 illustrates the final display. The experiment can be repeated with other filter parameters in order to explore how filter parameters affect output image quality.

8.6 Filtering impulsive noise using linear filters

Impulsive noise is a type of noise which is specifically characteristic for digital imaging systems. As indicated in chapter 5, impulsive noise results in the replacement of values of randomly, with a certain probability of error, selected pixels by random gray levels in the image dynamic range or with binary equiprobable gray levels of the minimum and maximum of the image dynamic range. In the latter case, noise is called *pepper and salt noise*, as it appears as isolated contrast white and black dots in images. The main problem in filtering impulsive noise is the detection of distorted pixels. When distorted pixels are detected, their gray levels are replaced by values obtained by means of one or another averaging of gray values of non-distorted pixels in their neighborhood. This is justified by the fact that normally gray levels of adjacent pixels do not differ much from one another.

In the exercise, methods for filtering general impulsive and pepper and salt noise are demonstrated in cases when locations of distorted pixels are known or unknown.

For the case of known locations of distorted pixels, two filtering methods are compared: (i) iterative band-limited DCT domain restoration, as in band-limited image reconstruction from sparse samples studied in chapter 3, and (ii) simple replacement of distorted pixels by an average of gray values of non-distorted pixels in their 3×3 neighborhood. In the band-limited restoration, the image DCT spectrum is limited by a pie sector with area equal to the rate of non-distorted pixels multiplied by image area.

For the case of unknown locations of distorted pixels, the two following filtering methods are compared.

1. Iterative filtering, in which, at each iteration step, the detection of distorted pixels is first performed by comparing the difference between the gray level of each pixel and the average over its 3×3 neighborhood with a detection threshold. Then pixels detected as distorted are replaced by the average over those pixels in their 3×3 neighborhood which were not marked as distorted at the detection stage. The detection threshold is proportional to the standard deviation of the difference signal; the proportionality factor is a user-defined parameter. The number of iterations is also user defined.

2. Recursive filtering, which is performed in the process of image scanning row-wise/column-wise. In this process, for each current pixel, a difference DIFF between its gray level and the average AV over its four neighboring already processed pixels (three on the preceding row and one preceding pixel in the current row) is compared with a detection threshold. If this difference exceeds the threshold, the current pixel gray level is replaced by the above average plus or minus (depending on the sign of the difference DIFF) an edge preservation threshold ('residual edge contrast'). Both the detection threshold and the edge preservation threshold are user-defined parameters of the algorithm.

At the start of the exercise, the user is prompted to select, as test image, either a prepared image, or any other image from the user's image database. Then the user has an option to select one of two types of noise: 'general impulsive noise' or 'pepper and salt noise'. For both types of noise, the user is then prompted to set the probability of error for noise simulation and the number of iterations for the iterative denoising filter, that assumes known positions of distorted pixels. For unknown positions of distorted pixels, the detection threshold and the number of iterations for

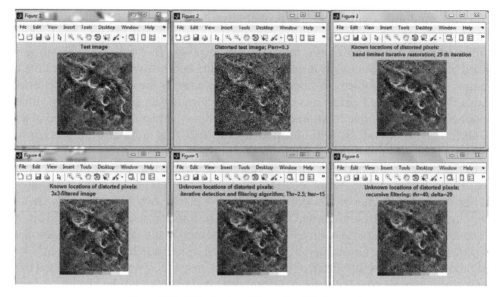

Figure 8.14. Filtering impulsive noise: filtering results.

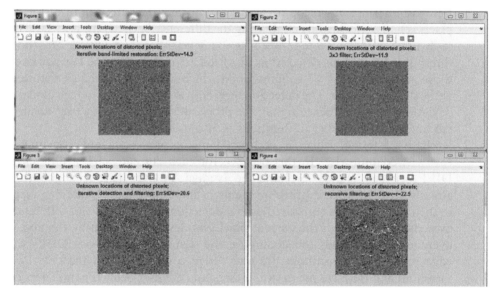

Figure 8.15. Filtering impulsive noise: filtering errors.

the iterative filter, and the detection threshold and the 'residual edge contrast' for the recursive filter, are to be set by the user.

The filtering is carried out in real time: filtering results are displayed, along with initial and noised test images, in the process of obtaining them. At the end, an option is offered of displaying differences between initial non-distorted images and filtered ones (filtering errors). Examples of final displays are presented in figures 8.14 and 8.15.

8.7 Image denoising using nonlinear (rank) filters

The main acting engine of the above filters is linear filtering (i.e. weighted summation, for each pixel, of pixels in its spatial neighborhood) for generating filtered image pixels or measures for deciding, when it is required, whether pixels are distorted. Theoretically, nonlinear filters, being a general case, may have higher image denoising potentials. An important subset of nonlinear filters is that of *rank filters*, which generate image pixel estimates on the basis of image local order statistics or histograms. Exercises of this section demonstrate the image denoising capability of two particular rank filters.

The first filter is the so-called *mean-EV filter* for image cleaning from additive noise. This filter works in a moving window of a certain dimension as the above local adaptive linear filters do, and generates estimates of pixel gray levels as a mean value over the pixels' *EV-neighborhood*. Window dimensions and borders of the EV-neighborhood are user-defined parameters. For better efficiency, the filtering is carried out iteratively, using, at each iteration, the image obtained at the previous iteration. The number of iterations is also a user-defined parameter. Mean-EV filters are most efficient at cleaning noise with a limited dynamic range, i.e. noise with values in a limited range [−Min, +Max]. If the range is known, its borders can be taken as borders of EV-neighborhoods. In the program designed for this exercise, the noise dynamic range is symmetrical with respect to zero (Min = Max). This range is also a user-defined parameter. At each filtering iteration, the program displays in real time of processing the noised input image, the output image, their difference and a graph of the standard deviation of the difference as a function of the iteration number. As test images, two prepared piece-wise constant images are suggested. The user can load for testing another test image from his/her image database as well. A sample of the final display is presented in figure 8.16.

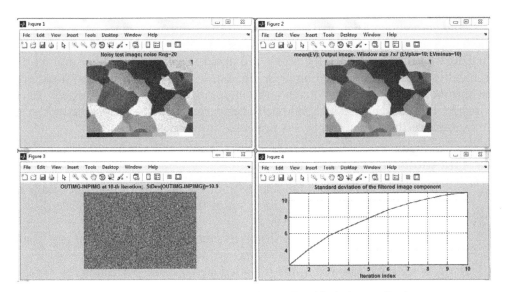

Figure 8.16. Mean-EV filtering additive noise of limited range (Rng).

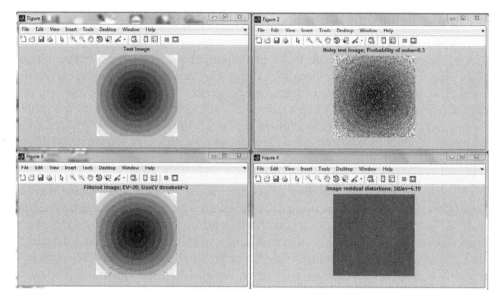

Figure 8.17. Impulsive noise cleaning using Size-EV neighborhood as a distorted pixel detection parameter.

The second exercise demonstrates a rank filter for cleaning impulsive noise. The filter works in the window of 3×3 pixels and uses for detecting distorted pixels a parameter *Size-EV*, which, for each pixel, is the number of window pixels that belong to its EV-neighborhood. The borders of the EV-neighborhood are a user-defined parameter. When this number is lower than a certain user-defined detection threshold, the pixel is considered as being an isolated outburst and its gray level is replaced by the average of those pixels of its 3×3 neighborhood which are not found to be distorted. The program works in two passes: detection of distorted pixels (first pass) and correction of detected pixels (second pass). As test images, three prepared test images are suggested, though the user can test any other image from the image database as well. At the start, the user is prompted to select a test image and set the probability of error for simulating noise, the borders of the EV-neighborhood and the threshold size of the EV-neighborhood for detecting distorted pixels. Each experiment can be repeated with modified filter parameters to achieve a better result. An example of the output displays is presented in figure 8.17.

8.8 Questions for self-testing

1. How would you explain the reduction of the number of non-zero beans in histograms of images after correction of their nonlinear gray scale distortions (see figures 8.2 and 8.3)?
2. How sensitive to noise in the distorted signal is the correction of gray scale image distortions?
3. How sensitive to noise in the distorted signal is the correction, by inverse filtering, of the imaging system frequency response?

4. Is there any difference between the results of moiré noise filtering in DFT and DCT domains? Explain.

5. What is the major drawback of global Wiener denoising filtering?

6. How would you compare the image denoising and deblurring capabilities of ideal and empirical Wiener filters for high signal-to-noise ratios? Explain the reason for your conclusion.

7. Why might noise variance estimation factors larger than one be required for successful empirical Wiener filtering?

8. If you compare results of global and local adaptive image denoising filtering, what distinctions do you see first?

9. What recommendations can you formulate for selecting window size for local adaptive denoising filters?

10. Explain the reason why maps of local filter transparentness are similar to those of image local standard deviations, such as shown in figure 5.3.

11. Why do local adaptive denoising filters exhibit an edge preserving capability?

12. How can one interpret images of difference between noisy input and filtered images from the point of view of the characterization of filter performance?

13. Does the Mean-EV image smoothing filter exhibit an edge preserving capability?

14. When locations of distorted pixels are known, what filtering do you find more efficient in suppressing impulsive noise: iterative filtering that generates band-limited approximations to images, or simple filtering by means of the replacement of distorted pixels by the average of non-distorted pixels in their 3×3 neighborhood? Explain the reason for your decision.

15. Does the optimal value of the threshold size of the EV-neighborhood for detecting distorted pixels in the Size-EV-based impulsive noise filter depend on the probability of pixel distortions (probability of error)?

16. On what property of images do the optimal borders of the EV-neighborhood depend in the Size-EV-based impulsive noise filter?

Chapter 9

Methods of image enhancement

9.1 Introduction

Image enhancement is processing aimed at assisting professional image analysis and facilitating image-based decision making. This usually requires certain purposeful distortions of row images, such as emphasizing some details and eliminating others, displaying hidden pixel attributes, making details which are invisible due to low contrast or other factors visible, visualizing numerical image parameters, outlining borders of objects etc. Image enhancement is an essentially interactive process carried out under expert user control.

The representation of images in a digital form provides practically unlimited opportunities for the implementation of all variety of image enhancements. Exercises collected in this chapter represent methods for the two most frequently required types of image enhancement: contrast enhancement and edge extraction. The exercises are listed in the entrance menu presented in figure 9.1.

9.2 Contrast enhancement

The following four methods of contrast enhancement are suggested for study: *unsharp masking, Pth law image spectrum enhancement, P-histogram equalization* and the *method of local cardinalities*. The first two methods enhance image contrasts by means of the amplification of image high-frequency spectral components in the transform domain, and specifically the DCT domain. The last two methods display pixel attributes other than gray levels, specifically pixel ranks and cardinalities, which also result in image contrast enhancement.

For all exercises, a set of prepared test images is suggested. The use of any other images from the user's image database is possible as well.

9.2.1 Unsharp masking

Unsharp masking is one of the earliest methods of image enhancement, that dates back even to the pre-computer era. It consists of displaying for visual analysis the difference

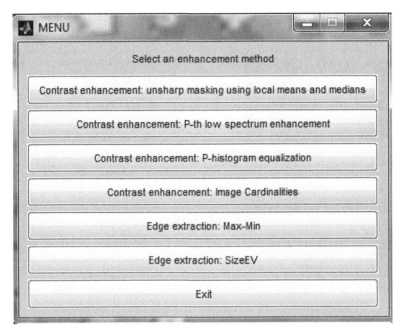

Figure 9.1. Methods of image enhancement: entrance menu.

between the image and its unsharp (blurred) copy generated by one or another image smoothing method. Due to this subtraction, low-frequency components in the image are eliminated or weakened, and, therefore, the weight of image low-intensity high-frequency components in the image spectrum is correspondingly amplified.

The two simplest and fastest image smoothing methods, smoothing by local mean and local median, are implemented in this exercise. They were demonstrated in chapter 5.

Upon selection of a test image from the list shown upon the program start, the user is prompted to set the X and Y dimensions of the smoothing window, and the program displays, along with the initial test image, its differences from the local mean and local medians computed in the selected window. These differences are enhanced substitutes for the initial image. Also displayed is the difference between local means and local medians themselves, in order to illustrate their distinctions for different images. An example of the final display for this exercise is presented in figure 9.2.

9.2.2 *P*th law image spectrum enhancement

*P*th law image spectrum enhancement is also an image enhancement method that redistributes image energy in favor of its high-frequency components. This is achieved in this method by means of raising absolute values of image spectral components to a power $P \leqslant 1$. The method can be applied both globally to the entire image spectrum and locally in a moving window. The exercise allows evaluation of the efficiency of both versions in applications to various pre-prepared images or to images from the user's image database.

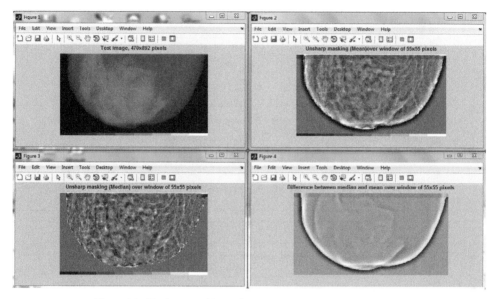

Figure 9.2. Unsharp masking using local image means and medians.

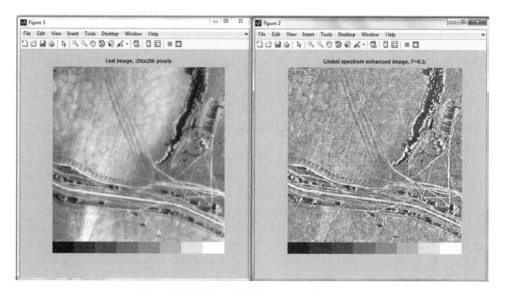

Figure 9.3. Pth law global spectrum enhancement.

For global spectrum enhancement, the user is prompted to specify the spectrum enhancement parameter $P \leqslant 1$, and the program displays, side by side, the initial image and the enhanced one (figure 9.3).

Local spectrum enhancement is supplemented in the exercise with an opportunity to simultaneously suppress additive noise in images using a local adaptive filter similar to that studied in chapter 8. Hence, it requires, in addition to the spectrum

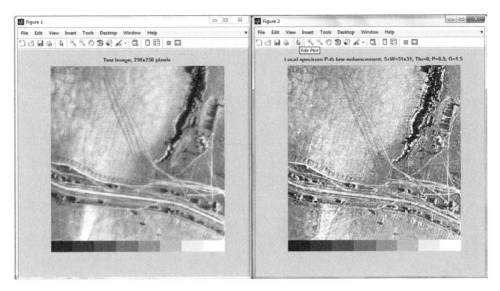

Figure 9.4. Pth law local spectrum enhancement.

enhancement parameter $P < 1$, specification of the sliding window X/Y dimensions, filtering threshold and spectrum amplification factor $G \geqslant 1$. The latter multiplies the Pth law modified local spectral components left after thresholding. An example of a final display is shown in figure 9.4.

9.2.3 *P*-histogram equalization. Pixel cardinalities

P-histogram equalization and *pixel cardinalities* are contrast enhancement methods that deal with pixel ranks and cardinalities as pixel attributes. *P*-histogram equalization is a generalization of the popular method of image *histogram equalization*. In histogram equalization, pixel gray levels are replaced according to a look-up table built by the cumulative summation of the image histogram. In *P*-histogram equalization, the look-up table is built by the cumulative summation of the histogram bins raised to a power P, which can be any real number between zero and one. The case $P = 1$ corresponds to regular histogram equalization. When $P = 0$, the actual pixel gray level range is linearly stretched to the entire image dynamic range 0–255. Intermediate values of P provide a kind of 'softened' histogram equalization.

The method can be applied both globally and locally. The parameter P and, for local P-histogram equalization, window X/Y dimensions are user-defined parameters. For global P-histogram equalization, displayed are the initial test image, the resulting image and plots of the initial image histogram and of the transformation look-up table (figure 9.5).

For local P-histogram equalization, displayed are the initial and resulting images (figure 9.6).

An alternative contrast enhancement method using image histograms is computing and displaying image cardinalities, i.e. the replacement of pixel gray levels by their cardinalities, i.e. by the number of pixels that have the same gray level (with the

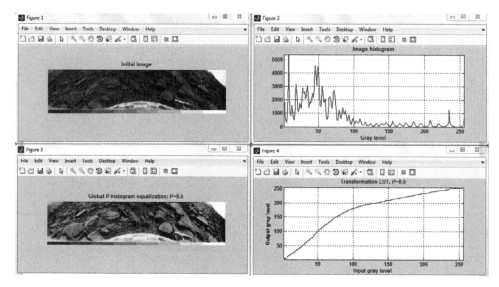

Figure 9.5. Image global P-histogram equalization.

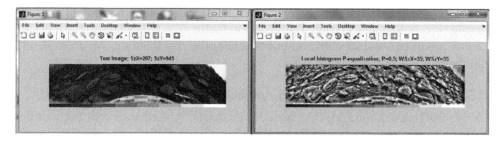

Figure 9.6. Image local P-histogram equalization.

corresponding normalization). This can be applied either globally to the entire image frame (figure 9.7) or locally in a moving window, as illustrated in figure 9.8.

For some images, the results of displaying image local cardinalities are more suitable for viewing displayed in a compressed dynamic range. This option is offered at the end of the exercise. For image dynamic range compression, the Pth law function with $P = 0.3$ is applied to image gray levels.

9.3 Edge extraction. Max–Min and Size-EV methods

Edge extraction is a very popular subject in image processing. Similarly to image enhancement, edge extraction is processing aimed at extracting from images their components that carry information on object borders and displaying this component for visual analysis. There are numerous edge extraction methods. Most of them are sensitive to the orientation of borders. In this section two robust, insensitive to edge orientation and simple, methods are suggested for experimentation, the Max–Min method and the Size-EV method.

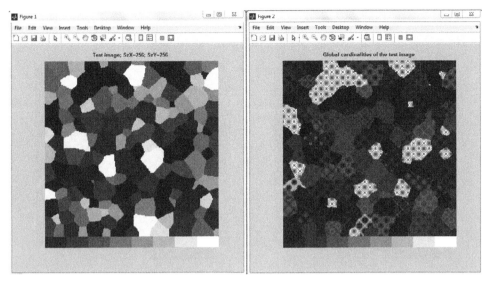

Figure 9.7. Image global cardinalities. The pattern seen in the processed image has too low a contrast to be visible in the initial image.

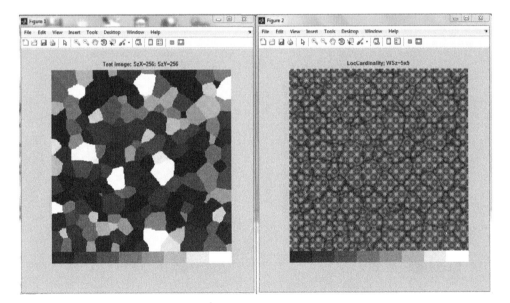

Figure 9.8. Image local cardinalities.

The Max–Min method consists in computing differences between maximal and minimal gray levels in a moving window. The Size-EV method consists in computing the number of pixels that form, in a moving window, the EV-neighborhood of the window central pixel. For the Max–Min method the program requires setting vertical and horizontal dimensions of the moving window. For the Size-EV method, it is necessary to set, in addition to the window dimensions, upper and lower borders

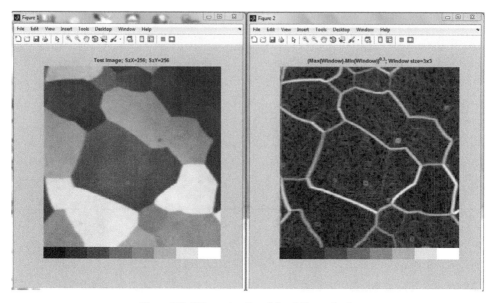

Figure 9.9. Edge extraction: Max–Min method.

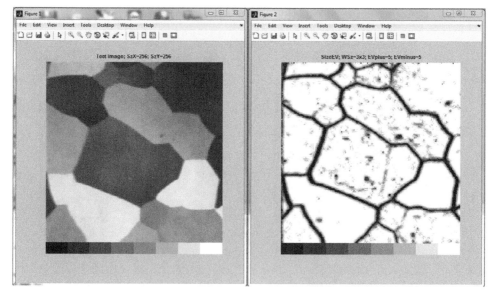

Figure 9.10. Edge extraction: Size-EV method.

of the EV-neighborhood. Both programs display the initial test image and the edge extraction result. Because these results may have a very large dynamic range, which hampers their proper display, an option is suggested of displaying the results in a compressed dynamic range, as in the previous exercise for image local cardinalities. Examples of final displays are illustrated in figures 9.9 and 9.10.

9.4 Questions for self-testing

1. In what sense do unsharp masking and Pth law image spectrum enhancement improve the image suitability for analysis?
2. What is common and what are the distinctions between the unsharp masking and Pth law image spectrum enhancement methods?
3. Does unsharp masking have any association with correcting imaging system transfer functions?
4. What are the distinctions in appearance of images obtained by unsharp masking using local means and local medians?
5. Why does P-histogram equalization result in the enhancement of contrasts?
6. Does displaying pixel cardinalities exhibit any edge extraction capability?
7. How does the appearance of edges extracted by Max–Min and Size-EV methods depend on the window size and, for the Size-EV method, on the borders of the EV-neighborhood?
8. Can the local cardinalities method be regarded as a special case of the Size-EV method?

CPSIA information can be obtained at www.ICGtesting.com
Printed in the USA
BVOW11*2232071014

369918BV00001B/1/P